IDAHO

By Robert O. Beatty

Published By

THE IDAHO FIRST NATIONAL BANK

IDAHO

Concept, editing, and text: Robert O. Beatty
Layout and design: Dale T. Ott
Photography: See page 204
Lithographed and bound in the U.S.A. by
The Caxton Printers, Ltd., Caldwell, Idaho
First Edition: October, 1974
Second Printing: April, 1975
Library of Congress Catalogue Card Number: 74-11819
ISBN 0-9600776-1-8

FOREWORD

The Idaho First National Bank came into being in 1867 just four years after Abraham Lincoln created Idaho Territory from a vast wilderness. For over a century we have grown up with Idaho and its people. We are especially proud of our ancestors and their accomplishments in shaping the destiny of our State, making it possible to be what it is today. We thought it time to tell the story in a memorable way worthy of our common heritage.

This, then, is our effort to combine and present the observations of many admirers of Idaho who have been nurtured by its heritage, refreshed by its beauty, and are faithful to its motto: *Esto perpetua* – "Let it endure forever." To them we dedicate this work.

We hope you enjoy viewing the book as much as we did creating it.

Thomas C. Frye
President

CONTENTS

INTRODUCTION

Producing a book about Idaho is like writing the first paragraph of the first chapter of a work with an infinite number of pages. The investment is in the creation. The profit comes from the pleasure others may receive in sharing the result.

If there is any merit in this book, it is due more to the ingredients and to the recipe than to the "cook." It is not an attempt at a precise and complete description of the state — historically, scenically, agriculturally, industrially, recreationally, or any other way. Rather, it is an effort to give the reader an honest feeling of what the land of Idaho and its people were and are all about. It is the distillation of impressions — visual, visceral, and verbal — over many years, some by those who know this state far better than I, but none who love it more. No one moves into Idaho and no one ever will. Idaho moves into you — when you're spitting snow; or the aspens shiver in an autumn breeze; or the wind down a hot canyon caresses your face; or you laugh at the glimpse of a golden eagle soaring, and gasp at a snow-capped mountain peak in the glory of a sunrise.

I have simply tried to add to that old story a touch of chutney here, or a little curry there and, perhaps, give those who know the state and those who will come to know it, a fresh way of thinking about and looking at what remains one of the truly lovely regions of America.

It is also a fact that in these hypertensive days, we need the refreshment of nature — the vigor, the beauty, the solitude, the sounds, the odors. Idaho is blessed with a lot of these. Whether we toil like dumb animals and pass them by depends only on our awareness and the aliveness of our own spirits. To say, "I haven't time . . ." to watch a sunset, or listen to a stream, or ski a mountain trail in powder is the ultimate disdain for the values of living here. These things are not inexhaustible, and with the rapid increase in people and their wants, it takes great restraint sometimes just to leave things alone.

Today the state faces the inevitable challenges of growth and discovery which began with Lewis and Clark and are accelerating each year. There is still time to plan its future and avoid the mistakes of so many others. As one Idahoan puts it, unless we do we are going to find ourselves in the not too distant future "with a lot of scrambled golden goose eggs."

The effort to produce it will have been worthwhile if this book helps, just a little, to encourage those here, and those who will come, to cherish Idaho's grandeur, its diversity, its rugged character and its self-renewing potential. Indeed, our common future and quality of life depend on it.

Robert O. Beatty
The Shallows
June 29, 1974

THE EARLY DAYS

The early days of Idaho began in an age of geologic upheaval a billion years ago. The state's startling contrasts in topography and natural beauty are due to the prodigious natural forces which shaped its mountains, its waterways, its valleys, and its high desert plains. Evidence of volcanoes and glaciers in its ancient rocks indicates little difference from the present day in climate or conditions. Over half of the state is between 5,000 and 10,000 feet in elevation, and there are 81 named mountain ranges within its borders. This has all been recorded in proper scholarly fashion elsewhere. Here we simply "show-and-tell" briefly how Idaho came into being, try to give a little feeling of what the country and its people looked like in the beginning, what they look and feel like now, and why.

For at least 150 centuries before the empire builders, the West belonged to the Indians. The record of how the white man took Idaho away from them is no better, nor worse, than anywhere else. In 1803 Thomas Jefferson arranged for the U.S. to buy what is now Idaho from Napoleon Bonaparte for three and three-fifths cents an acre. That's a shade under $2 million — not a bad deal, even with inflation! Idaho was about one twentieth of the package. History books call it the "Louisiana Purchase." It secured what Jefferson considered essential to the future of the Republic — a continent stretching from "sea to shining sea," and from the Great Lakes to the Gulf of Mexico.

For 60 years Idaho was variously a part of several vaguely defined protectorates, comprising those states now generally referred to as "The Northwest." When Abraham Lincoln finally gave it the dignity of territorial status on March 4, 1863, Idaho included all of what is now Montana, most of Wyoming, and parts of the Dakotas and Nebraska. How it got carved down to its present fairly respectable size of 83,557 square miles isn't really important. What *is* important is that over the 171 years since it has been a part of the

A Pictorial Overview of IDAHO

world's greatest experiment in individual liberty, some of that freedom still remains. Idaho is no longer frontier, of course, but the old frontier still lives within its borders here and there, and many new challenges are facing its citizens — more awesome in many respects than unbreached mountain ranges or untamed rivers.

Students of semantics and inventors of legend have come up with a variety of origins for the word "Idaho," from the name of a side-wheeler steamboat plying the Columbia River, to Indian mythology. No one really knows for sure. The tale I like to perpetuate is that I/da/ho is a contraction of the Shoshone words, "Ee-dah-how," translated to mean everything from "gem of the mountains" to an ancient exclamation: "It's morning!" as the sun came up and tinted the diadem of the mountain peaks with pink and gold. At any rate, during the early 1860's, when Congress was cutting up the western territories into all kinds of combinations, the name "Idaho" won out over "Montana" due to the action of a senator from Massachusetts, who cared little and never even visited the place.

There followed an incredible series of human adventures — beginning with Jefferson's commission to the explorers, Meriwether Lewis and William Clark. They were followed shortly by the fur traders and trappers, and then the wagon wheels rolling west with the missionaries, the miners, the homesteaders, the farmers, the ranchers — all following the trail to the fabulous Oregon country. And finally, modern Idaho, less than a generation old, really, with its tomorrows more alluring than its yesterdays.

Stephen Vincent Benét, in *Western Star*, summed up the mood of the human spirit which settled the West and which persists in Idaho today:

> *"Hear the wind*
> *Blow through the buffalo grass,*
> *Blow over wild grape and brier.*
> *This was frontier, and this,*
> *And this, your house was frontier."*

There were for generations before the whites and still are, five distinct Indian groups in Idaho. Three (the Kootenai, the Coeur d'Alenes, and the Nez Perce) live in the north, and two (the Shoshone and the Northern Paiute-Bannock), in the south. They survived here 15,000 years or more, eating roots, rabbits, fish, mountain sheep, deer, birds, and whatever else they could lay ahold of with primitive tools, snares, and weapons. There were even buffalo roaming the southern Idaho plains until 1840. A staple sugar-producing food was the bulb of the lovely "quamash" or "camas" lily. Thousands of years before the rise and fall of Babylon, people were digging the roots of this plant on what is still known in Idaho as Camas Prairie. For centuries it was a gathering and harvesting place. Its vital importance triggered not only intertribal warfare but also battles with the white settlers, who were interested in plowing up the camas meadows to plant grain and hay. Beginning with Lewis and Clark, many a pioneer subsisted for long periods on camas cakes, which they received as gifts from the Indians or made themselves. There are still camas meadows scattered about the state to remind us of those early days. Their rich blue flowers, massed in a remote meadow or along a back-country byway, are a delight to the eye.

Idaho Indians now live mostly on reservations — Fort Hall, Nez Perce, Duck Valley, Coeur d'Alene. For 75 years after the Shoshone helped Lewis and Clark across Idaho, the Indians fought to retain what they had, by their standards, owned for ages. Totally ignorant of the concept of deeded land, they were classed as savages. Our forebears, fighting to possess what they considered free for the taking, were proclaimed by the missionaries of all faiths as splendid soldiers of God. The Indians were assassins. No wonder the credible redmen were, at times, confused by the Whitmans, the Spaldings, the Youngs — and many like them — who came to convert the heathen to Christian brotherhood and the Golden Rule. Somehow it inevitably resulted in the Indians' giving up their ancient homelands for a pittance — or for nothing.

The first recorded footprints of the white man in Idaho were those of a tall, blond, 29-year-old assistant to the President of the United States. Chosen by Thomas Jefferson to fulfill a remarkable dream of exploration and empire, his name was Meriwether Lewis. His spelling and grammar were a bit uncertain, and his manners were stiff and awkward, but he had a "firmness and a perseverance of purpose which nothing but impossibilities could divert from its set direction." Jefferson wheedled $2,500 from a diffident Congress for the expedition.

On August 12, 1805, Lewis halted his party to rest just east of the Continental Divide at what is now Lemhi Pass. One of his men, McNeal, stood astride an eastern flowing rivulet, and exulted that he had lived to see the headwaters of "the heretofore deemed endless Missouri." That night Lewis wrote in his journal: ". . . we proceeded to the top of the dividing ridge, from which I discovered immence ranges of high snowcapped mountains still to the west. . . . I now descended about three quarters of a mile . . . to a handsome, bold running creek of cold, clear water (Horseshoe Bend Creek). Here I first taisted the waters of the great Columbia River." This must have been a thrilling moment in an epic of exploration unmatched in the history of our nation. How the explorers knew it was the Continental Divide is a mystery, but they knew.

Lewis and Clark carried with them a medal, struck especially for the expedition, with the President's bust on one side and a handshake, a peace pipe, and a tomahawk on the other. This, along with other trade goods, they bartered with friendly Indians for much needed food, horses, and directions. An unsuccessful attempt to navigate the turbulent Salmon resulted in its description as the "River of No Return." So they retraced their steps, headed north, recrossed the Continental Divide at Lolo Pass, and followed the Lolo Trail through Idaho to Oregon and the Pacific — and back again in 1806 by essentially the same route.

Kulleyspell House and the fur trappers and traders

were not far behind. In contrast to permanent settlement, white occupation of Idaho occurred first in September, 1809, on lake Pend d'Oreille with a "house for trading," built at the mouth of the Clark Fork River where it enters the lake. The post was built by David Thompson, with the British-owned Northwest Fur Company. Northwest headquartered in Montreal. It and the Hudson's Bay Company dominated the Idaho fur trade for 30 years. As late as 1923, a blind Kootenai (Klai-too — "old Alec") was able to guide Duncan McDonald, a descendant of Finan McDonald, Thompson's partner in the venture, to the precise site of the ruins.

The object of it all was a rodent, with a fur prized for hats and a glandular secretion, castoreum, prized as a cure-all for everything from colic to hysteria, and also used, even today, as a fixative in perfume. The beaver's engineering skills and abilities as a timber cutter are legendary. The men who trapped them were a tough lot, freebooters whose principal law was survival. They lived life with relish, grieved little over what was gone, wore greasy buckskin breeches blackened by many campfires, and strode with danger so constantly that fear was an emotion they scarcely understood. Many took Indian maidens, with or without the consent of the tribe. Many Indian girls were lithe and strikingly beautiful, more fastidious in personal cleanliness than most frontier white women, and quite willing to share the buffalo robe of an attentive and lonely trapper, no matter how weatherbeaten he was or how badly he smelled. One of the last of the mountain men in Idaho was "Beaver" Dick Leigh, who married a lovely Indian girl named Jenny, settled down, and raised a family in the Teton Valley.

The fur trapping era in Idaho was generally peaceful. Indeed, most of the trappers lived pretty much like the Indians, and white exploration and trade did not seriously disrupt Indian political, social, or cultural institutions. That came later with the miners, the ranchers, and the farmers.

They came by the thousands, following a 2,000-mile trail often called "the longest cemetery in the nation." More than 250,000 of them tried it between 1840 and 1862, averaging one burial for every one-tenth mile. 'We're agoin' West — we don't know where we'll bring up at!" was the common cry. Much of the Oregon Trail is covered today by highways and city streets, but here and there you can still see the ruts made by the wheels, pulled by oxen, mules, horses — and, sometimes, people. There were many wonders en route, like the balanced rock, about ten miles south of the trail. A popular ford across the Snake was Three Island Crossing, above Glenns Ferry. In 1836, Mrs. Whitman wrote: "There is one manner of crossing which husband has tried, but which I have not, neither do I wish to. Take an elk skin and stretch it over you, spreading yourself out as much as possible. Then let the Indian women carefully pull you out on the water, and with a cord in the mouth they will swim and draw you over. Edward, how would you like to travel in this way?"

Zane Grey immortalized the wild mustang in his book about a great red stallion called "Wildfire." A hundred movies have embellished that romantic tale. Certainly, though, the wild West and the wild horse are synonymous. We will all lose a little if they disappear. As with all wild things, the pressure is on. Idaho has a few scattered bands of mustangs — about 250 in Owyhee County, and another group of about 150 in the Salmon and Lost River mountains near Challis. An estimated 45,000 wild horses and burros still roam the western states. The trouble is they eat grass, like cows and sheep, and are, therefore, quite controversial, like the coyote. Many an Idaho rancher would agree, I'm sure, with cattleman Mike Hanley that the best solution would be to train coyotes to eat mustangs and vice versa. To me, the thundering hooves of a band of mustangs still sound better than the splutter of a motorbike. If we "manage" these animals into extinction, we will lose forever a bit of the renewable richness of Idaho. I hope we're not that grass-poor yet.

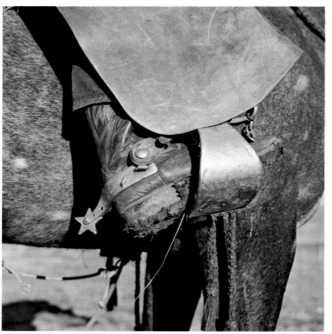

Below: Freight wagons, Mountain Home, 188
Emmett Stage to Thunder Mountain mines, 190
Wickahonney stage stop, Owyhee
Right: The wheels of fortune rest at Silver City min

The Oregon Trail entered Idaho at its southeastern corner, and followed the Snake River west to Farewell Bend, just upstream from the impassable Hells Canyon. A great many Oregon trailers turned south to California at Soda Springs, or down the Raft River lured by gold at Sutter's Mill and by land sharks who came as far north as Fort Hall, near Pocatello, to divert settlers south. Starting with the "Forty-niners" and influenced by the discovery of silver and gold in north Idaho in 1860 and in the Boise Basin and the Owyhees in 1862, the California trail, north and south, carried a larger volume of traffic than any in the West. Much of the Idaho portion of both the Oregon and California trails continued in use for stage and freight service to the mines long after the Civil War and the coming of the railroad. It was a dramatic saga of men, women, and wheels — an incomparable mixture of courage and chicanery, unmatched in the opening of empires. Shakespeare's "Fortune, good night; smile once more; turn thy wheel" could have been the universal prayer.

CAPTAIN E. D. PIERCE

The trappers were solitary men and sought the farthest reaches of the frontier because they loved it. Quite different, the early miners. Of the thousands who poured into Idaho in search of riches, many were petty thieves, shysters, and restless unfortunates, part of a feverish and floating horde, who rushed from strike to strike with visions of wealth bright in their eyes and a willingness to do almost anything to get it. With some exceptions, they were a rough crew. They swore like pirates and drank whiskey as though they had been nursed on it. Occasionally one, like Jack Stoddard of Silver City, hung on to his mine, married, started a sawmill and a cattle ranch, and built a fancy house to show the world that he had "arrived."

Will Bassett, of Captain E. D. Pierce's prospecting party, started it all on the eve of September 30, 1860, with the discovery of placer gold in substantial quantities on a tributary of the Clearwater River in north Idaho. Said Pierce: "We found gold everywhere in the stream . . . I never saw men so excited. They made the mountains ring with shouts of joy!" From that moment, the course of Idaho's history was inevitably altered. In a period of 20 years, 20,000 men, and a very few women, scrambled into the mountain citadels and pounded, panned, sluiced, or otherwise extracted by various methods, fortunes in gold and silver. Elliott's *History of Idaho Territory,* first printed in 1884, reported that in just 20 years the gold and silver production of the Territory was $100,290,530.14. There is no record of who got the 14 cents. Quite possibly it was Will Bassett!

The strikes, and the towns which grew up around them in the Boise Basin, in the Owyhees, and in north Idaho are legendary — Atlanta, Florence, Gilmore, Bayhorse, Yankee Fork, Smelterville, Custer, Roosevelt, Pierce, Kellogg, Stibnite, Thunder Mountain, Delamar, Silver City, Placerville, Buffalo Hump. The principal population center of the Northwest in the 1860's was Idaho City with 30,000 residents. Its mines produced more gold than all of the Klondike. The old U.S. Assay Office in Boise, built in 1871 and

Below: Borah home, Boise, built 1895

Borah fishing Idaho Primitive Area, 1927

Right: Trial scene, June 1907;

Orchard (1), Darrow (9), Haywood (11)

Below Right: Pettibone, Ada County jail, 1907

Governor Frank Steunenberg, 1900

Clarence Darrow at the trial, 1907

James H. Hawley, 1925

Hawley and Puckett law office

at Thunder Mountain mines, 1901

still standing, confirmed more fortunes and dashed more dreams than any comparable facility in the world, and is said to have processed at least $75 million in dust, nuggets, and ore samples in ten years.

Colorful participants in the early days of Idaho were the Chinese. Willing to work for less — almost slave labor, in fact — industrious, and clannish, a census in 1869 showed that the majority of Idaho miners were Orientals. Supported by the San Francisco tongs, they left their mark on the state and on the course of empire, not only in mining but also in railroading. Chinese joss houses (temples) existed in Boise until very recently. The early miners, who got $1 to $2 an ounce, would have boggled at gold's bringing $160 an ounce, as it has recently. At that price, even with inflation, the day may come again when miners will walk the streets of the decaying towns and rattle the bones of the ghosts.

Idaho's early mining era encouraged a lot of shootings, hangings, and other assorted skulduggery. The most notorious deed, the killing in 1905 of a former governor, stemmed from the lust for precious metals beneath her soil. By the time the trial began in May, 1907, in the old Ada County court house, the case was a national issue involving President Theodore Roosevelt and his Secretary of War, William Howard Taft. In the courtroom it pitted legal giants against one another, and produced eloquence unsurpassed in the annals of American jurisprudence — Senator William E. Borah and James H. Hawley (later governor), for the prosecution; versus Clarence Darrow, legendary champion of lost causes (e.g., the Skopes "monkey" trial on evolution and the Loeb-Leopold kidnap and murder case), for the defense. Murdered by a bomb in his Caldwell home, former Idaho Governor, Frank Steunenberg, had held that office from 1897-1900 during the mine uprisings and violence in the Coeur d'Alene country to the north. Conditions were so bad he declared martial law and sent in the militia. A bronze sculpture of Steunenberg, erected in 1927, still stands, facing the state capitol building in Boise.

Accused as the assassin was a drifter named Harry Orchard, who confessed to the crime and to having been hired to accomplish it by the Western Federation of Miners, under big Bill Haywood, leader of the International Workers of the World. Haywood got his start as a miner in the 1860's in the famous Trade Dollar mine at Silver City in Idaho's Owyhee mountains. (See page 111 for color photo of this mine today.) He and his codefendants, George Pettibone and Charles Moyer, were imprisoned in Boise.

The case created a national sensation. Socialist Eugene Debs, in a hair-raising speech in Chicago, entitled "Arouse, Ye Slaves!," attacked the "monsters of capital" for jailing his comrades. Teddy Roosevelt, stirred to anger by the breakdown of law and order, got into a running battle with the entire American labor movement, as well as with Maxim Gorky, the renowned Russian revolutionary and novelist. Mass demonstrations of thousands were organized against Roosevelt in Chicago, Boston, and New York.

Labor raised $300,000 by popular subscription to retain Darrow. His eleven-hour defense oration secured the acquittal, on a technicality, of Moyer, Pettibone, and Haywood (who is now buried in the Kremlin). Orchard was sentenced to life imprisonment.

Borah, the silver-maned "Lion of Idaho," while a controversial man, had previously gained considerable popularity in a classic court case in 1896, where he had eloquently obtained suffrage for the women of Idaho. He went on to a distinguished career in the U.S. Senate, including chairmanship of the Senate Foreign Relations Committee, but retained his love for Idaho and its beauty throughout his life. The state's highest peak, 12,655 feet, is named in his memory.

Jim Hawley, the pioneer attorney who started in a tent at the Thunder Mountain mines, served two terms in the Territorial legislature, as U.S. Attorney, as mayor of Boise, and finally as governor in 1911-12. Giants all — men of courage and frontier spirit that have lasted long after they died, and set Idaho apart today.

All of Idaho's early conflicts did not revolve around mining. Another western trademark, the classic range wars between cattlemen and sheepmen, was a part of it too, and some notorious characters evolved from them. In what is now Cassia County in southcentral Idaho, the cattlemen, in a desperate stand, established Deadline Ridge across the entire county, declaring no sheep dare pass the line. In 1906 several bands of sheep were found "out of bounds," and not long afterward two herders were found dead, with .44-calibre slugs well placed in each. The triggerman was identified as a swaggering, articulate young cowpoke named "Diamondfield" Jack. He was convicted (with William E. Borah as prosecuter for the state), later acquitted at the eleventh hour just ahead of the noose, (with James H. Hawley for the defendant), and wound up selling gold mining stock in Nevada at 20 cents a share. Jack's mining ventures made him wealthy and respectable, but he died an inglorious death in Las Vegas in 1949, struck by a taxicab.

Another early Idaho character was the second Territorial Governor, Caleb Lyon, of Lyonsdale, New York, appointed by Abe Lincoln in 1864. As the photo shows, he wanted to go down in history in good company, but like many early fly-by-night Idaho governors, his interest wasn't in governing, but rather in personal gain.

Lyon held office for two years. He was a studious easterner, who had applied to be U.S. Minister to Bolivia, but wound up as Governor of Idaho Territory and as Commissioner of Indian Affairs. The Bolivians got the best of the deal! Lyon negotiated a treaty to acquire the Boise valley and the Owyhees from the Shoshone. Because no one could put a price on the purchase, the U.S. Senate never got around to ratifying it. Lyon left Idaho in 1866, with little to show for his stay except $46,418.40 — the entire undisbursed Indian fund for the Territory! Described as "egotistical, ambitious — a scholar, a poet, and an art lover, but a conspicuous and dangerous failure as an executive," he hardly helped the chaotic condition of Idaho's affairs at that time.

There were noted women, too — like Mesdames Marcus Whitman and Henry Spalding who, in 1836, were the first white females to cross the continent. Spalding's daughter, Eliza, was the first all-white child born in Idaho. Her Presbyterian missionary father established Idaho's first school and church at Lapwai to serve the Nez Perce. The courage, vigor, and endurance of these pioneer women, and the thousands who followed them, were extraordinary.

Like "Pegleg" Annie Morrow of the mining camp of Atlanta. Rough miners amputated both of her frozen feet at the ankles with a meat saw one winter, with a few slugs of whiskey as an anesthetic for all parties involved. She lived for many years thereafter. Then there was horse queen, Kitty Williams, who in the 1880's raised horses by the thousands at her Bruneau ranch for the eastern markets. She was Idaho's most famous woman of that period. Statuesque and lovely, Kitty could ride better than most men, but she dressed to the teeth in the latest Parisian fashions when on trips to the Eastern horse markets.

With the opening of the Idaho mines, navigation of the Snake River became of great consequence. From the West, travelers caught a stern-wheeler up the Columbia to the Snake to Lewiston. Getting beyond there to the Boise Basin and Owyhee mines by water through Hells Canyon seemed more attractive, if possible. Several attempts were made to run steamers that far upriver. The Oregon Steam Navigation Company even built the steamer *Shoshone* at Fort Boise in 1866 with such service in mind. Incredibly, she made it all the way to Walter's Ferry above Swan Falls, and then downstream again through Hells Canyon in what must have been one of the wildest rides for a boat of that size ever attempted. But the coming of the railroad and improved stage travel finally ended this heroic effort in early water navigation, though for many years steamers served the interior to Lewiston without difficulty.

Ferries were a bit different and a vital part of early transportation and immigration. They were generally privately operated, and most of them took their names

24

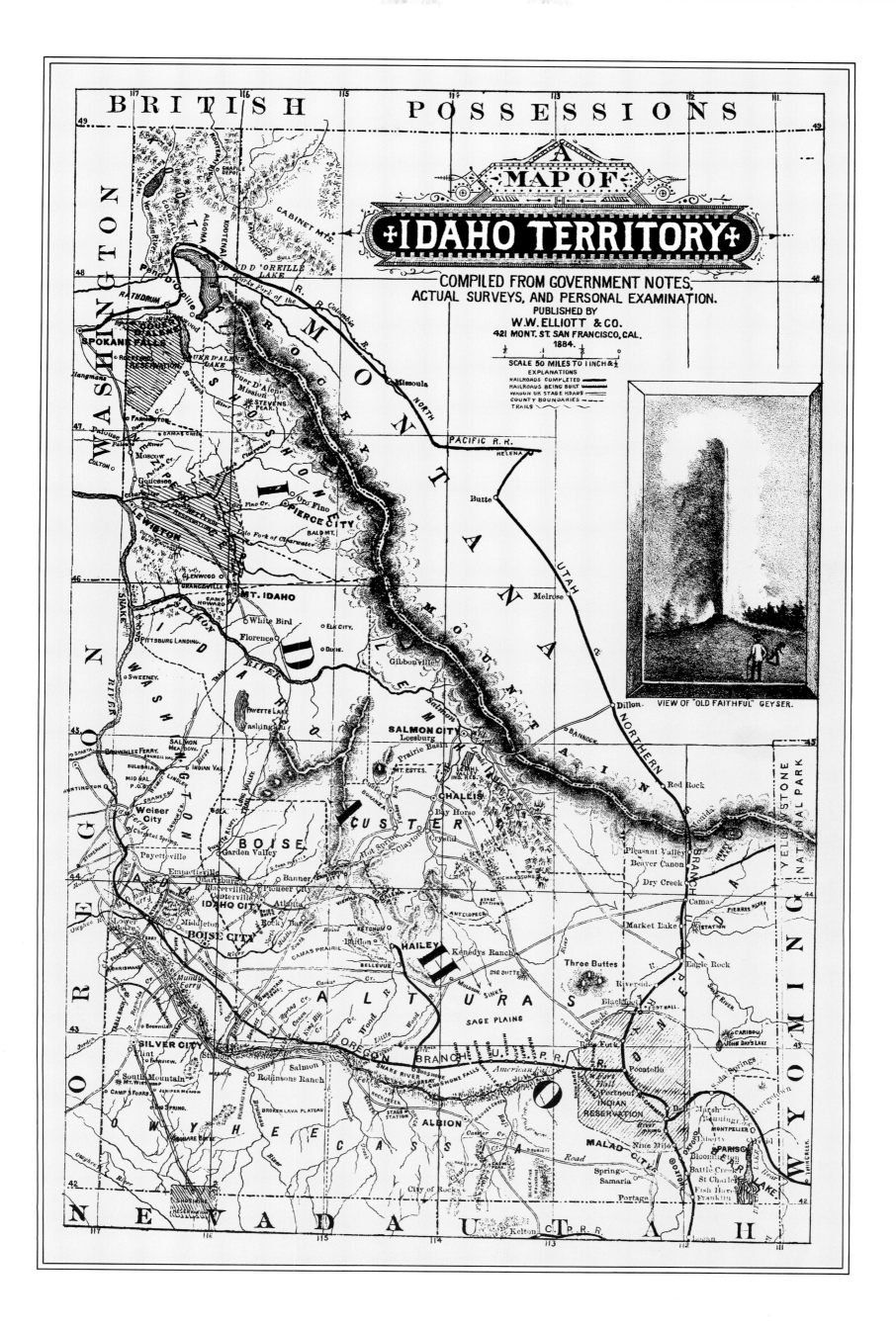

A MAP OF +IDAHO TERRITORY+

COMPILED FROM GOVERNMENT NOTES,
ACTUAL SURVEYS, AND PERSONAL EXAMINATION.
PUBLISHED BY
W.W. ELLIOTT & CO.
421 MONT. ST. SAN FRANCISCO, CAL.
1884.
SCALE 50 MILES TO 1 INCH & ½

EXPLANATIONS
RAILROADS COMPLETED
RAILROADS BEING BUILT
WAGON OR STAGE ROADS
COUNTY BOUNDARIES
TRAILS

VIEW OF "OLD FAITHFUL" GEYSER.

from the men who built and ran them to carry wagons, livestock, and people across otherwise impassable waterways. To ferry a wagon and a horse cost 50¢.

The "iron horse" reached Idaho via the narrow gauge Utah and Northern Railroad, from Brigham City, Utah, to Franklin in 1873. In 1887, 262 miles of its track, from Pocatello to Garrison, were converted to standard gauge in a single day, one of the most dramatic events in railroad history. The Northern Pacific laid its lines across north Idaho in 1880 to 1882, and the Union Pacific (Oregon Shortline) completed its tracks across south Idaho a year later.

The coming of the railroad was the beginning of the end of frontier life as the pioneers had known it — and most of them welcomed the change. Along with it came the interurban trains and streetcars — all part of a bygone era of colorful transportation.

Even so, waterways were still used as a means of transport for resources, even as late as 1971. That year saw the last of the log drives and their colorful

"wanigan" supply rafts down the Clearwater River. The drives ended with the construction of Dworshak Dam.

To open the West, the railroads, in general, and the Union Pacific, in particular, were motivated by an act of Congress, which granted each road ten alternate sections of land (6,400 acres) along their rights-of-way for every mile of track built. Later the grants were doubled so that the railroads received free some 19 million acres of Jefferson's great buy from Napoleon, with the right to do with it as they wished, including selling it to land-hungry settlers. This, coupled with the Homestead Act of 1862, was the fuse that set off the explosive agricultural settlement of the West, including Idaho. Productive mining land was also a hoped-for bonus. Land speculators poured in by the hundreds and the land-hungry settlers from the East, by the thousands. One famous land rush near Pocatello, starting at noon on a bright day in 1901, threw open an expanse of ground, purchased from the Indian tribes at Fort Hall, for $1.25 an acre. All one had to do was to run out, stake his claim, and then somehow get to the Government Land Office at Blackfoot, 21 miles away, to record it. Fortunately, the Oregon Shortline ran a special fast train from McCammon to Blackfoot, via Pocatello, for the stakers. The trip took 54 minutes. W.D. Sweeney, via horseback, beat the train by one minute, however, and filed the first claim in the Fort Hall mining district at 12:55 p.m.

Many who got their land made it in one way or another — and many did not. Idaho is strewn with picturesque old cabins, which, if they could talk, would tell quite a story of "hurry-up" and heroism and hope. It wasn't all work and hardship, of course, and once in awhile the folks went skiing or fishing, but more often than not there was a purpose other than pleasure behind the effort — like eating, for instance. It seems incredible today that anyone would try to ski in the outfits shown to the left, but they did about 1915 and it looks as though they are enjoying it.

As for the fishing, there was a day when you could catch a white sturgeon in the Snake River that literally

took a horse, a mule, or a Model T, pulling on all four cylinders, to land. The specimen of this giant fish, shown here, was caught near Twin Falls in 1908. It was 11 feet long and weighed 632 pounds. Others taken from the Snake have weighed more than half a ton! White sturgeon still reside in Hells Canyon and in the Swan Falls-Guffey reaches of the Snake. They live to be 100 years old or more, but are today protected as a rare and endangered species.

By 1885 the pioneers of this sparsely populated region had begun to understand the richness of the sagebrush plains and the northern prairies. Wheat crops, producing three to five times as many bushels per acre as Illinois, Virginia, or Tennessee, astounded them; and men like Anders Hoidal from Norway, a "giant in the earth," who helped settle the Palouse country near Troy in 1880 made it happen, when horsepower rather than tractor-power was the only supplement to manpower. Fruit orchards of all kinds were started, the Payette River valley around Emmett being a prime spot. Plantings of apples, cherries, peaches, and pears reached 20,000 trees a year by 1880, and many orchards produced 40,000 bushels of fruit each year. Grapes were tried too, but did not take hold till much more recently. Everything else seemed to grow in abundance. The *Idaho World,* reported that "Mr. and Mrs. Potts from Boise valley came to town last Thursday with a load of vegetables. Many of his cabbage heads would weigh 20 pounds, and all were nice and solid." And on Camas Prairie in 1883, the meadows, once deep blue with camas lilies in the spring, were producing 250 bushels of grain per acre with irrigation, and 100 bushels without it.

They used to haul spuds to the depot in 100-lb. gunnysacks on horse drawn wagons. In those days, people bought, peeled, and mashed their own Idaho potatoes. Today, great trucks dump their loads onto the conveyor belts of huge processing plants, and 80 per cent of the product coming out the other end is in boxes, dehydrated or frozen. The peelings are used to fatten beef cattle.

Left: Mason jar magic, then and now
Below: Homestead kitchen, Homedale, 1904
Land Rush, Milner, near Twin Falls, 1909
Abandoned dream, Teton Basin, 1972

Below: Anders Hoidal, Palouse pioneer, 1937

Doorway to the past, Caldwell

Shipping potatoes, Blackfoot, 1890's

Harvesting oats, Idaho Falls, 1906

Right: Wheat field, in the shadow
of the Tetons near Driggs

These industrious farmers and ranchers; the woodsmen who came in to log Idaho's great forests and the miners who still dig riches and metals from the earth in Idaho's fabulous Coeur d'Alene district — they are the people who have shaped the state's present and will strongly influence its future.

In the beginning, they were in a hurry and seldom aware of how their works were changing the face of the land. After all, there was so much of it — and a man has to eat, doesn't he? So, where the mountain men once trapped fur, rippling grain now grows chest high; and vast fields of potatoes and sugar beets, onions, fruit and other produce for the markets of the world.

But the winds of change are blowing hard and fresh breezes are stirring not only the quaking aspen but also the attitudes of people, even in relatively remote Idaho. Whatever the future holds, the purple mountain majesty, under the autumn clouds, will remain; and each morning the rising sun will crown the peaks in a glory of light — even as in the early days.

Left: "Les Trois Tetons"
Below: Quaking aspen

THE BORDER ROCKIES

For 312 miles, the eastern border of Idaho is the Continental Divide. Although Idaho has 81 named mountain ranges of its own, its story would be incomplete without the Rocky Mountains.

Perhaps no other range of the Rockies is so storied as those named by the original male chauvinists, the French voyageur-trappers who helped open the American West. These great granite "breasts," the Grand Tetons, are well within the visual boundaries of southeastern Idaho. They provide an outstanding example of alpine topography, and an infinite array of opportunities for human experience. Three of them, "Les Trois Tetons," have been landmarks for man from prehistoric times. As seen on pages 33 and 34, they display many moods and seasons.

In 1835, Indian missionary Samuel Parker wrote about them in his journal: ". . . I spent much time in beholding the towering mountains . . . sometimes filled with emotions of the sublime. I descended . . . much gratified with what I had seen of the works of God." To anyone seeing the Tetons, they are "exposed forever on the sensitive emulsion sheet of one's mind." Much of the special character of Idaho's Rocky Mountain borderland comes from its proximity to these magnificent "hills" and from the peoples who, for thousands of years, have gathered their strength therefrom.

The Teton Range was the eastern backdrop for the famous rendezvous of the early mountain men. Known then as Pierre's Hole, this gathering place for trappers, traders, and Indians might more appropriately have been named "Hell's Hole" in light of the fighting and debauchery that occurred at these renowned summer bacchanals. Today Idaho's Teton Basin is a broad and beautiful valley where man peacefully tills the earth. Quaking aspen line the creeks and still serve as the principal food and building material for the remaining beaver — the furry "gold" that first lured white men west and opened up new empires.

Sturdy descendants of these hardy trappers and of Oregon Trail immigrants grow livestock, grain, and potatoes in Pierre's Hole now. Saturday night in Driggs, Tetonia, or Victor isn't much different from any other village in America, except for sunset on the spectacular mountains nearby, where chipmunks still scamper through pine and fir. The mountain scenery is unchanged from the legendary days of Jim Bridger, Kit Carson, Jedediah Smith, and "Beaver" Dick Leigh, who trapped and camped here.

In 1810 a group of Missouri Fur Company traders under Andrew Henry established a winter post, called Henry's Fort, near what is now St. Anthony — the first American establishment in the Pacific Northwest. The name is immortalized in Henry's Lake and the Henry's (north) Fork of the Snake River — two of the more famous fishing waters in Idaho. In 1822 Henry and William Ashley established the first successful commercial enterprises in what is now Idaho — the Rocky Mountain Fur Company. In four years they retired back to St. Louis as wealthy men, wearing stovepipe hats of beaver felt!

Today the Henry's Fork is a fishing stream, watering a fertile valley. On their way to the sea, these waters flow in shimmering cascades, oft-spangled with sunbows, over two of Idaho's loveliest falls — the Mesas. Upper Mesa, the more spectacular, is born from a vertical drop of 114 feet. These pristine waters flow initially from Big Springs which gushes from the earth a full-fledged stream, providing ideal conditions for the landlocked sockeye salmon, or "kokanee," to spawn, turn red, and die. A picturesque old well house still graces Big Springs, built over 40 years ago in this poetic setting by an immigrant German cabin builder, Johnny Sachs. Johnny is long since gone. Let's hope the cabin will remain.

Big Springs drains into a scenic irrigation reservoir in the center of the lovely Island Park plateau at the foot of the Centennial Range. It is a fine fishing lake and home for myriad waterfowl. A less important, but amusing, fact is that Island Park village (pop. 136) boasts

37

"the longest main street in America" — some 30 miles — due to a 1947 Idaho law which permits sale of intoxicating beverages only in incorporated communities. As a result, some Idaho villages take in more real estate than most big cities! The early mountain men would have appreciated such convenient spirits in the back country!

Just south of Island Park is the 11,000-acre Railroad Ranch which the Harriman family, of Union Pacific fame, has willed to the people of Idaho for state park management and ultimate public use. This crown jewel of the high parkland forests, not yet open to the public, contains some of the loveliest scenery and the best fly-fishing in the state. The ranch occupies a major portion of an extinct volcanic caldera, 26 miles in diameter, and is a treasure trove of prehistoric human and animal activity in the area for at least the last 12,000 years. Its bird sanctuary is a nesting place for the rare trumpeter swan, page 42, enjoying early morning solitude on the Henry's Fork. Railroad Ranch

is, literally, a home on the range where "the graceful white swan goes gliding along, like a maid in a heavenly dream." A few miles east of the ranch is Yellowstone Park. When first established as a territory in 1863, Idaho included *all* of what is now Yellowstone Park. About 31,000 acres remain within the boundaries of this remote corner of the state. There are no roads and few trails, but if you hike in some summer you might see an Idaho elk in Yellowstone, taking his ease at Robinson Lake meadows!

It seems fitting that a state with so many mountains should have the Mountain Bluebird as its state bird, so voted by the school children of Idaho in 1929. Unique among bluebirds, the male has a cerulean breast, like an Idaho sky. I've seen them everywhere. Their short song suggests the caroling of a thrush. The bluebirds were here long before mountain men harvested the beaver and miners dug precious metals from the mountains. They will remain, I trust, a harvest of natural beauty for a long time to come.

Preferred nesting locations include holes in old trees — perhaps in the lightning-killed snag of a great ponderosa pine among the forests that blanket the mountains all 'round. In early days, these trees were felled and dragged down to the mines by mule or oxen for cabins, tunnel timbers, flumes, and, most importantly, to make charcoal for the smelters. Huge mule-drawn freight wagons rolled tons of charcoal to the mines of Idaho for smelting lead, gold, and silver. The charcoal was made in beehive-like, stone kilns shown here. You can stand inside one, looking out the entrance toward the Bitterroots, another of Idaho's Rocky Mountain ranges. In the 1880's sixteen others like it served the smelters at Nicholia, which produced a fourth of all the lead mined in the U.S. Nicholia has long since disappeared, as has most of the silver mining town of Bayhorse — the principal remains of which are the crumbling kilns seen in the other photo. Thirteen million dollars in silver came out of a vein there, discovered in 1872 by a prospector looking for — guess what? — a missing bay horse!

While the abandoned kilns are a mute and colorful testimony that most of the precious metals are gone from this area, Idaho's border Rockies are still being "mined" — today by those seeking solace, solitude, and outdoor recreation, laced with crackling mountain air. Alpine or cross-country skiing at Grand Targhee, on the west slope of the Tetons, will fill your face with some of the finest powder snow in the world and "blow your mind" with scenery. Hunting, camping, backpacking, fishing, pack-tripping, ski-touring, or just plain looking now make up an important part of the "gold in them thar hills" that the prospectors of earlier days would have found difficult to comprehend.

By 1889 the border Rockies area was getting populated enough so that Harry Gordon, fresh from Michigan, homesteaded a cabin, fished through the ice in Henry's Lake, and the first winter sold his catch of cutthroat trout for 5 cents a pound. "Somedays we

caught a thousand fish apiece," he wrote home. "I plan to haul out my own fish and make big money." Gordon, a confirmed bachelor, stuck it out until 1893. The price of fish had risen to 7 cents a pound, but the cost of his loneliness had risen higher. In his last forlorn correspondence he wrote, "Are there any single ladies around there looking for straws? If so, send them West. There ain't a single lady between 20 and 60 in this country that hasn't got a dozen or more men on the string!" He concluded, "Tomorrow's my birthday and I wish someone would tell me how old I am. It is a fact I do not know!"

In this time-pressure age, I sort of think that if I could live in the Henry's Lake basin the year-around, birthdays would not be a concern, in spite of cold weather!

And rough-hewn fur trader, Andrew Wyeth from Boston, might have laughed at a lovely flower named after him, the wild wyethia, or "mules ear," which abounds about the borders of Henry's Lake. The wyethia is sometimes also called "compass plant" because its

leaves were thought to point north and south. Its roots were an Indian food. The lake contains shrimp, and produces some of the fastest growing trout in the West.

Idaho's eastern border leaves the Continental Divide at Lost Trail Pass, and turns westward along the crest of the Bitterroot Mountains. Here is the focus of a major headwater collection point for thousands of waters which, like the Teton drainage far upstream, flow westward into the mighty Snake, the Columbia River, and the sea. Perhaps the best known of these is the Salmon "River of No Return," shown here in its upper reaches but a quiet stream in autumn. Take the time to stand by it for awhile, and watch its waters dancing in the light, as it tumbles over boulder and shallow.

"The pace of autumn quickens," said David Cavagnaro. "The golden trees blaze. Another season cycles past, but the stream flows on and on . . . embraced by the meadow in its turn, and the sea and clouds in theirs, and man in his."

Indeed that could be the life story of Idaho.

BEAR RIVER BASIN

Idaho was first permanently settled by whites in the Bear River basin. A redoubtable band of Mormon pioneers in antelope skin pants and beaver hats started the Bear River settlements and, despite wilderness circumstances of the most forbidding and discouraging nature, they hung on. These early followers of Brigham Young left their stern but courageous imprint on Idaho, still noticeable today.

Few Mormons of those days suffered the same problems of winter loneliness as did Harry Gordon of Henry's Lake basin, noted earlier; but they did have one thing in common — the severe winters, survived in crude log cabins like the one at Gray's Lake (left). Jim Poulsen, a settler of Paris, Idaho in 1863, said of the area: "This is a hell of a country! It's so cold in the winter it freezes the milk in the cows' bags and so hot in the summer you can't sit on a rock without scorching the seat of your pants!"

The region is storied in history. From Bear Lake west to the Nevada line and north to the Snake River, it was the gateway to the Northwest from the eastern U.S. and the main wagon train access to and from Oregon and California. Bear River and the lake connected with it were so named by Donald MacKenzie, leader of a Northwest Fur Company brigade to the region in 1818. Most of the bears are long since gone, but Idaho's first town, founded in 1860 on the Utah border, the village of Franklin, is still there (pop. 420).

Today it is a hay, grain, livestock, and phosphate mining country. The picturesque towns and villages have all the modern comforts. But less than a hundred years ago, meat meant a sage hen, a jackrabbit, an antelope, a crane, or a mule deer. The "venado burro," so known in Mexico for its great donkey-like ears, is the most wide-ranging big game animal of the West. It is not easily fooled by the average weekend hunter. Indeed Aldo Leopold once said, "There are four categories of outdoorsmen today: bird hunters, duck

Left: Newly hatched sandhill crane
Below: Adult crane defends nest
Polyphemus silk moth

hunters, deer hunters, and non-hunters. They represent four diverse habits of the human eye. The bird hunter watches his dog, the duck hunter watches the skyline, the deer hunter habitually watches the next bend, and the non-hunter does not watch!''

As the bucks shed velvet from their antlers and the fall mating season draws near, the deer gather in bands of 6 to 10. A group of them against an early snow, coats shining proudly in the sun, presents a superb picture.

There are lesser mountain ranges — the Caribous, the Wasatch, the Portneufs — but the character of the country is molded by high-altitude valleys, most of them over 5,000 feet. These have, in turn, fashioned the character of their residents — the plants, the animals, and the people who first took root here.

The sandhill crane, once thought to be on its way to extinction, nests in Gray's Lake National Wildlife Refuge. Basically a huge marsh, the Refuge is a principal breeding ground for these great birds which present a unique avian spectacle. The rust-colored young, just hatched, look like fuzzy full-grown ducks. Adult birds weigh as much as 14 pounds and stand 4½ feet tall! In summer I've had them stalk "crawking" through my camp in the evening. The novice stares in disbelief and asks, "Are they *always* that big?" Yes. Experienced naturalists have even mistaken them, at a distance, for deer.

The lesser (smaller) variety of crane has returned to huntable numbers in the southwestern U.S., but no hunting is permitted for the greater crane, whose total Rocky Mountain population is estimated at 12,000. In the early days crane on the table was considered a delectable feast, sometimes bringing $18 to $20 per bird for Christmas dinner in San Francisco!

There is, however, no closed season on the silk-spinning polyphemus moth — if you can catch one! These night flyers live in Idaho too, and if you think a giant sandhill crane can generate a sense of wonder, you should see a giant silk moth with the afterglow of evening on its wings!

Some of the first irrigation techniques in America started in 1855 with a series of small ditches at Lemhi, eastern Idaho, to convert the wild grasses and weeds into cropland. One is still in use. The settlers of Franklin expanded the activity. Reclamation in southeastern Idaho began in earnest in 1863, with a company whose name would warm the heart of a bait fisherman — the Worm Creek Canal Company. A ditch was built 15 miles long at a cost of $30 thousand. It watered 15,000 acres. Less than 100 years later, in 1958, Palisades Reservoir was completed on the South Fork of the Snake River at a cost of $45 million! It provides water for 720,000 acres. Idaho gets its agricultural reputation from many similar efforts.

Some say that the weed will win in the end, but I think that even weeds bring a harvest of beauty and utility. The dried teasel pictured here gets its name from the fact that it was used in the early days to "tease" up the nap on homespun wool. So, until the weeds take over, the water brings new life, beauty, and re-creation to the high desert. It is worth the cost if we don't give up too much of our natural land and wildlife heritage to get it. The end of such choices is fast approaching.

Above: Teasel
Right: Palisades Reservoir
Overleaf: Bear Lake with wild geese

The most prominent feature of Idaho's Great Basin is Bear Lake and the river that flows from it. People living for 150 miles around call themselves "Bear Lakers," underlining the influence of these waters. A dyed-in-the-wool Bear Laker will turn rhapsodic over the countryside and the lake. Writes one, ". . . Bear Lake, 8 miles by 20, green as the spring, blue as the sky, clear as a mirror, and as changeable as a woman's mind. Its valley raises the finest strawberries and raspberries this side of paradise!"

Half in Idaho and half in Utah, Bear Lake is a gift of the primordial glaciers — not man. It is home to a unique fish, the Bonneville cisco — a silvery little member of the whitefish family found nowhere else in the world. The spring spawning run of cisco into the shallows occurs in mid-January. It triggers a major festival and is a magnet for fishermen from all over the region. Thousands line the shores or chop holes in the ice and harvest as many as half a million of these tasty creatures with long-handled dipnets. Rolled in meal and fried in deep fat, or smoked over hickory chips, a Bear Lake cisco is hard to beat!

Much of the character of early Idaho was shaped by the fortitude of its settlers who came in ox-drawn wagons, on foot, or pulling handcarts — seeking freedom in "the promised land." They had to contend with harsh weather, scarce food, and marauders of all types. In 1863 Idaho's largest Indian battle occurred near the Bear River — a confrontation of over 200 Army cavalry and 550 Shoshone. This was the historic homeland of the northern Shoshone and northern Paiute (Bannock) Indians. They variously helped or harassed the westward movement of the white man. There were numerous "massacres" by both sides. A series of treaties finally settled the Indians on the Fort Hall Indian Reservation in 1868. The town of Pocatello is centered in the Reservation and is named after a Shoshone chieftain. Literally translated, the word means, "Po (road) ka (not) tello (to follow)." Apparently few people paid much attention to the name, since today Pocatello is the second largest city in Idaho.

Even before the homesteaders were the mountain men, like David Lewis, a trapper-explorer with the legendary Jim Bridger. Lewis came west as a boy of 18 into what is now Idaho for $50.00 a month, plus gun and ammunition, "if you shoot yer own meat." His descendants operate a ranch near Elba today, and he was buried, age 92, at Albion.

And Joseph Scarborough, who emigrated at age 11 from England to Salt Lake in 1861, the last 2,000 miles by oxteam. He helped settle Franklin, sired 11 children, and in 1900 built a classic Welsh-Victorian home from local bricks in what became known as "Mormon architectural style." It still stands, almost like new.

Another early Bear Laker, Mrs. Charles H. Hauck, was born on the Bear River in 1880. With her family she pioneered the settling of Wyoming's Big Horn basin. At the age of 20 she drove a wagon and team back along the Oregon Trail to Idaho, married, raised nine children, and ended a busy life at Idaho Falls. For all her rugged life, there's an aura about her that reminds me of the fragrance of the wild rose that grows in old tangled fence rows or by some unfrequented roadside. "A whiff of the wild rose," said David Grayson, "will bring back a train of ancient memories — old faces, old scenes, old loves, and the wild thoughts I had when I was young."

One of the most notable landmarks to immigrants was the City of Rocks. A camping place for wagon trains, the nine-square-mile basin of great granite spires presented a vista of bizarre splendor. One California traveler wrote in his diary in 1849, "The road continues around these rocky piles, church domes, spires, pyramids. In fact, with a little fancying you can see anything from the capitol at Washington to a lowly thatched cottage." Almo, nearby, was a favored spot for Indian attacks. Crumbling stone ruins are mute testimony that someone finally found a "city" to their liking and tried to settle there. At least a quarter million people followed these rugged trails through Idaho from 1840 to 1860.

Bridge, Idaho (elevation 4,740), just to the east, is, I'll wager, the only sod-roofed official post office still in use. The wagon trains originally crossed the Raft River here en route to the City of Rocks and California or Oregon. It serves a widely-scattered ranching population of 15, and proves that Idahoans just don't waste perfectly good old buildings! If one likes the wide open spaces, the best postal job in the United States would be postmaster of Bridge!

The Soda Springs are another pioneer landmark still much in evidence. The colorful mineral mounds and bubbling waters were well-known to the early fur trappers, as were the lava hot springs 40 miles to the west. Many drank the effervescent waters, wistfully reminded of rarely enjoyed beer or champagne. Wrote one early wagoneer, "The water is clear and has a smart taste like beer, though it has more of a sting to it than any beer I ever drank. I drank freely of it. It had a very good effect!" Many of the missionaries and immigrants described these remarkable boiling waters in great detail. Pioneer women found the water excellent for breadmaking in place of yeast.

The town of Soda Springs, formed in 1870, lies directly on the Oregon Trail and was an important junction point for the westbound wagon trains. The springs are not much different in appearance from when the settlers stopped and viewed them in awe and wonderment. The town has the only golf course in the world where one can lose a ball in the Oregon Trail, noticeable remnants of which run right through the ninth fairway!

This underground action of mineral springs is also responsible for the noted Lava Hot Springs, discovered in 1819, and today a highly developed spa. Undoubtedly related is the fact that the Bear River basin in the 1870's produced immense quantities of salt, for both the gold and silver smelting processes and as a condiment for the frontier diet. In the 1870's the Oneida Salt Works were one of the most valuable salt springs on the continent, annually producing 500 tons.

Today the world's largest phosphate deposits are found in the area, used for medicines, fertilizers, and a variety of purposes hardly imaginable by an immigrant, who wrote in 1846: "the Sody Spring is a quite a curiosity. Take a little sugar and desolve it in a little water and then dig up a cup full and drink it before it looses its fass. It is frristrate. I drank a hal of galon of it."

Much has been written about the West that isn't so, but it is a mighty land which has spawned strange events, powerful people, and many natural bounties. Like the cattail, for instance. Its roasted root provided food and flour; its leaves made baskets and chair bottoms, waterproof caulking, and a coarse sewing twine; its downy seed-hairs made fine insulation, a dressing for wounds, or a soft pillow. The greatest blessing, however, was the elbowroom, which seemed to foster respect and human concern.

Someone said that physical strength is measured by what we can carry — spiritual strength by what we can bear. The pioneers who settled the West, in general, and southeastern Idaho, in particular, displayed a fair measure of both. Bear Laker, Ezra Poulsen, writing recently about the impact of the lake on his life, said:

"To those of us whose destiny was planted by this fountain of pure water, comes a sense of indebtedness to a pioneer tradition, rough-hewn, but solid; insisting on an honest measure of good citizenship. If those with the talent and the inclination want to amass millions, build great cities, and shoot for the stars, that will be alright. Man was born to grow and master his surroundings as well as himself. Yet he still needs a cottage, a garden, a valley surrounded by friendly hills and mountains for periods of relaxation, planning, and thought; or, even more likely, to recover from the wounds incurred in his battles of conquest."

Idaho was, and remains, a place of discovery and conquest — all kinds. But more importantly, perhaps, a place where one's spirit can be perpetually refreshed by the sights and sounds of vigor, the titanic features, and the permanence of Nature, no matter how we use or abuse her.

THE SNAKE RIVER PLAIN

"Arriving at the summit of a small hill, we obtained for the first time a splendid view of Snake River. The scene was truly magnificent; by mutual instinct, both man and beast halted in rapturous admiration. Within a few miles we beheld as far as the eye could reach an expansive sheet of water, equally as wide as the Columbia; on one side an extensive sandy beach, on the other a pebbled strand, giving it all the appearance of a bay on the seacoast. In the foreground were rolling hills — at a distance the Boise, Payette, and Salmon Mountains, covered with snow. It was a sight seen but once in a life and then never forgotten."

So wrote a correspondent for a San Francisco newspaper in 1863, the year the Idaho wilderness was given territorial status. Early miners and homesteaders who traversed its grass and sagebrush wastes would have disagreed with such a glowing account.

The Snake River meanders for over 500 miles in a broad crescent through the plains of southern Idaho. En route it plunges over a dozen waterfalls, some higher than Niagara. The river has been called "the Nile of Idaho." Certainly it is the queen river of the Intermountain West — a somewhat bedraggled queen, to be sure, but not without marks of former splendor. At least half of the state's sparse population lives within 50 miles of the river, and in a very real sense survives because of its life-giving waters. The Snake watershed represents, by volume, about 40 per cent of the entire Columbia River system. Its 17 power and irrigation dams provide life and a living for millions — mostly outside Idaho's boundaries. But not without cost, and the trade-offs in any future development of this great waterway are, it seems, becoming more acute. One homespun Idaho poet has written, "When a river is named for the tempter of Eve, how fitting that she should be so many times dammed!" She finished her comment about the prodigal river by consigning the Snake to the chasms of Hells Canyon!

Others don't go quite that far, but pose the real question troubling many Idahoans today: "We need water (and power), it is true, but how many more dams must we build to power more cities and nourish more crops in order to support greater numbers of people who will only demand additional supplies of water?"

The French voyageurs called the Snake "La Maudité Riviére Enragé" — "the Accursed Mad River" — after their frail cottonwood canoes failed to conquer its many cascades, falls, and gorges. The name that finally stuck, however, came from the Indians. For ceremonial and sign language reasons, several tribes were grouped in early explorers' journals as the "Snake Indians." Their horses grazed on the abundant arrowleaf balsam root, still an important livestock forage. They also made their marks in many places up and down the river and its tributaries. One of the most noted aboriginal art "galleries" is the field of boulders laid down in the glacial age near Walter's Ferry, not far from Swan Falls canyon. Either chiseled in stone by

hammering (petroglyphs) or painted with colors obtained from minerals and plants mixed with grease and water (pictographs), these "doodlings" have no common form for sound or meaning. They are, in fact, the individual artistic expressions of their creators — possibly for magical or religious reasons, or possibly just for fun. One finds these art forms on rock all over the state. As yet no Idaho petroglyph or pictograph has been carbon-dated, but pictures of extinct animals and discovery of ancient tools indicate that Indians used the Snake basin for at least 10,000 years before the coming of the white man.

No doubt the sand dunes have been here that long too. You can fence in a cow or possibly a snowdrift, but it's difficult to fence in a sand dune on the move. The pioneers described southern Idaho as a desert, hopelessly unfit for permanent occupancy by white men. They may have been thinking of the sand dunes near Bruneau (over 300 feet high), or at St. Anthony, or others near Idaho Falls and Weiser. These striking

Left: Mallards, Hagerman Refuge
Below: Thousand Springs region
Right: Mormon Temple at Idaho Falls
Shoshone Falls

examples are partially residues from wind erosion which facets strange "ventifacts" in sandstone or other soft rock. Their basic reason for existence lies in what one county agent defines as an Idaho "rainstorm" — e.g., "two or three drops of water, a lot of wind, and then the sun comes out!" The Bruneau dunes cover 600 acres and have several fresh-water lakes, attracting myriad forms of wildlife — to say nothing of people.

Basque sheepherders from the Pyrenees might agree with George Bernard Shaw that in their home country "the rain in Spain falls mainly on the plain" — but not on the Snake River plain! This prompted an early opportunist from Portland, Oregon, to write Idaho Governor McConnell in 1894, "I can offer you three months' rain for One Thousand Dollars . . . at three inches a week. That's very cheap and more than some states receive in a year!" The Governor declined. So not rainfall, but snowfall, on the great mountain ranges to the north and south continues to provide the Snake River with most of its life-giving water. Much of the plain itself is a huge underground aquifer, where entire rivers vanish into the ground, to reappear as far as 250 miles away. All of the origins and outlets of this water puzzle geologists, but some are well-known. Major rivers in Idaho which disappear into the desert include both Big and Little Lost Rivers, Birch Creek, and part of Henry's (north) Fork of the Snake, itself. The aquifer includes underground ice caves, deep chasms, and great lakes buried in the porous lava.

The water reappears at such spectacular places as Malad Gorge and the Thousand Springs area of the lovely Hagerman Valley. Of the famed Thousand Springs, only four remain undeveloped for either power, irrigation, or commercial trout production, and there is currently a controversy over what is going to happen to one of these. The waters and cliffs here were viewed with awe by the early immigrants. For several thousand years before that, aborigines used the cliffs as animal jumps, over which they drove herds of range animals, such as bison and antelope, to their deaths. The remains of prehistoric fauna found in the Hager-

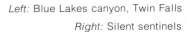

man area are among the most unique fossil sites in North America, now threatened by irrigation.

Nearby Salmon Falls on the Snake (formerly a salmon fishing site for the Indians), Twin Falls, Shoshone Falls (212 feet — 64 feet higher than Niagara), Idaho Falls, American Falls, most of them still spectacular cataracts today, support the voyageurs' name of "enraged river." Visitors still watch, listen to the roar, and the story they seem to tell of nature's power and endless bounty. We are beginning to realize, however, that it really isn't endless — that springs and streams and, ultimately, big rivers can run low on "fuel" — like campfires and eagles and stars — and even men, in time. The key word is "balance" among all the forms of life whose existence depends upon the river.

Dedication in 1971 of the Snake River canyon below Swan Falls as Birds of Prey Natural Area is foresight that benefits all. It was established "that the eagle, the falcon, and other raptors may soar free for man's inspiration." Idaho has one of the largest populations of golden eagles left in the West and the largest breeding population of prairie falcons known to man. This canyon is home, as well, to the bald eagle, the rare peregrine falcon, and other birds of prey. They live mainly on desert rodents and snakes, not cuddly little lambs! Indeed, current proposals to irrigate vast new sagebrush tracts on the plains above the canyon will destroy the ground squirrel habitat, and thus the food supply, for these great birds, imperiling their survival. The golden eagle and the rugged Snake canyon were selected for the dust jacket of this book because, together, they symbolize to me the fierce beauty, the majesty, and the free spirit of Idaho's past, its present, and its future.

Fifty million years ago a series of great lava flows dammed and diverted the Snake into new courses. This wild canyon home of the eagle and the hawk, and other great chasms, like the Blue Lakes canyon area at Twin Falls, were formed eons ago by the river cutting its way down through these massive lava flows, on its way to the sea.

Below: Prairie falcon
Morley Nelson with "Otis"
Birds of Prey Natural Area
Right: Wild golden eagle

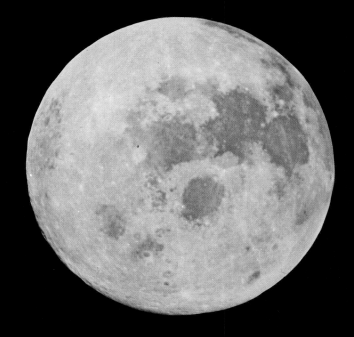

A most visible evidence of these flows is the startling Craters of the Moon National Monument. One early writer described it: "The panorama of this area at sunset is overwhelming. Few spots on earth have such power to impress the human mind with the awful inner nature of the huge rock planet on which the human race moves at incredible speed through the universe."

This 85-square-mile lava wilderness is a surface outcropping of the vast underground aquifer mentioned earlier. Washington Irving, in his journals on the adventures of Captain Bonneville, wrote, "The volcanic plain is some 60 miles in diameter. Nothing meets the eye but desolate and awful waste, where no grass grows nor water runs, and nothing is to be seen but lava." It's not quite that bad today. A surprising number of animals and plants inhabit what was, when formed about the time of Christ, a sterile wilderness. Included is the lovely bitterroot (*Lewisia rediviva*), the state flower of Montana, first collected by Meriwether Lewis in the Bitterroot Valley in 1805, and named after him. The "rediviva" part of the Latin name, meaning "brought to life," refers to the use of the root of this plant as food by the Indians. Spatter cones, seen everywhere, were formed by great gas bubbles, bursting through the surface of the molten rock cooking at 2000°. The monotony of this grotesque landscape is broken by the great cone of Big Southern Butte, looming on the eastern horizon. Pushed by volcanic eruptions to a height of 7,576 feet, it was a guiding landmark to the wagon train pioneers. These cones, crags, and craters strikingly resemble the surface of the moon, once seen by man only through a telescope. There is no more remarkable, nor more visited, geologic phenomenon in the state.

The extreme topographic contrasts in Idaho have produced great riches — not only precious metals and fertile soils but also scenic, too, from lofty jagged mountains, and deep canyons, to deeply eroded plateaus and rolling hills. With elevations from 700 to 12,662 feet, the state displays a unique diversity of face and form.

Left: Moon as seen from Apollo 16
Below: Bitterroot flower
Ropy pahoehoe lava flow
Spatter cones
Craters of the Moon wilderness

Left: Mating strut, sage grouse cock
Below: Antelope, Route 22, near Arco
Strawberry cactus
National Reactor Testing Station
and Twin Buttes through natural arch

Surrounding Craters of the Moon is the desolate sagebrush and cactus desert which, not far to the east, is home of the National Reactor Testing Station. To the immigrants toiling under hot summer suns, these plains of artemisia, with plants sometimes higher than the back of an ox, provided wearying obstacles.

A century later, in 1953, a 900-square-mile chunk of this wilderness, nearly the size of Rhode Island, was home to the first generation of electricity from nuclear power in the U.S. Over 50 nuclear reactors have been built at this "sagebrush campus," more than anywhere else in the world. Viewed toward the south through a remarkable natural bridge, the area remains principally the home of the sage grouse, the jackrabbit, and the antelope. Wagon trains, pushing westward through a sea of sagebrush sighted the Twin Buttes, in the distance, giving them some of the "goaheaditiveness" that sighting land provided early mariners.

In spite of such intrusions, the booming of male sage grouse still reverberates in the spring over rocky

Left: Windmill, waiting for an Idaho
"rainstorm" near Meridian
Below: Duck hunting, old Fort Boise

draws, down desolate alkali flats, sounding like distant cannon fire. First recorded by Lewis and Clark as "Cock of the Plains," this spectacular bird goes back at least 3 million years and, like the eagle and the hawk, is totally dependent on the survival of sagebrush wilderness. The same booming grounds are used year after year, and there are few more spectacular prenuptial displays of bird courtship in North America. The ceremonial dances of the plains Indians mimic these mating dances. Old-timers found sage "chickens" a welcome addition to the larder. They are still so regarded.

Elsewhere the waters of the Snake have converted the sagebrush plains to rich, arable land. You'd think that with all the wind in an Idaho "rainstorm," windmills would be a common sight, but inexpensive hydropower makes them more of a picturesque rarity, adding a touch of interest to the landscape. The water which nourishes vast crops has also attracted great concentrations of waterfowl and other birds. With all of

the out-of-staters moving in these days, it "ain't what ⟨
used to be," but a man can still frost his fingers in ⟨
duck blind of a morning, and hear the guttural feeding
chuckle of mallards settling into the decoys; or stan⟨
belly-high in a tributary of the Snake with fly rod hel⟨
high in tribute to a fighting trout; discover an old ha⟨
barn or purpled gorge; or travel a country road by ⟨
little spring that smiles and says, almost audibly
"Rest!"

"Nature," said David Grayson, "passes the dishe⟨
far more rapidly than we can help ourselves." How tru⟨
— and Idaho sets quite a table!

For some, a well-stocked table means these thing⟨
For others, it may mean thousands of bags of potatoe⟨
or onions, standing row-on-row in the fields, when th⟨
mountain maple is in scarlet and the cottonwood⟨
along the river bottoms are like piles of yellow bloom⟨
or a spirited Appaloosa filly, silhouetted against ⟨
weathered barn, almost like a Wyeth painting. T⟨
some in southwestern Idaho, it now mean⟨

vineyards, too, and an infant Idaho wine industry. Imagine Cabernet Sauvignon in the sagebrush!

Whatever the interest, water makes the difference. Extensive irrigation systems have changed the face of the land a good deal from the day when the region was described as vast desert tracts that must forever defy cultivation and interpose dreary and thirsty miles between the habitations of man. It's these volcanic plains, washed with snow water from the great mountains, which grow the state's most famous crop — potatoes. Although Idaho made the russet potato famous, it is now grown in other parts of the country. Any Idahoan will tell you, though, that good cooks know the difference!

The Boettcher hay ranch, just west of Fairfield, is a classic example of old-new Idaho. There Mary Lietz was born 65 years ago. She still lives there. Sixty-five Fairfield valley winters have left their mark on the buildings and on her, but beauty and character are visibly displayed by both. Like Mary, her horses and her build-

Left: Old orchard near Walter's Ferry
Below: "Plow deep and straight . . ."
Hops, Wilder
Peaches, Emmett valley

ings, hay from this valley is rough cut, perhaps, but all are "of the first water." "Character," said Bartol, "is a diamond that scratches every other stone." Mary Lietz is of the rough-cut diamond aristocracy of Idaho which helped turn the barrens into fertility. An old stanza, penned in 1843, sums it up:

> *"Ye rigid Plowmen! Bear in mind*
> *Your labor is for future hours.*
> *Advance! spare not! nor look behind!*
> *Plow deep and straight*
> *With all your powers!"*

But the plains without water, while never worthless, grow little to fill man's belly. A vast network of canals and ditches carries the snow "gold" of the Snake to water the high desert and has created the lasting riches of the Boise Basin. It all started in 1862, with the discovery of a tawny metal that stirred men's minds and bodies — indeed which has created and destroyed whole civilizations — gold! Mining was the prime mover, reclamation second, in the plans of the New York investors who hoped to use the water from canals to work Snake River placers in the summertime, following irrigation. That scheme was good for only a couple of million dollars of powdery gold from the Snake itself, but it started the New York Canal, among many others, and made an agricultural paradise out of a desert. It also created the occupation of ditchrider, whose job it was to ride the canals with a sharp eye and a shovel, patching gopher holes and other leaks which let the precious liquid escape. Thomas William Patton retired as one of these, working for the New York Mining and Canal Company. He came to Idaho in the early 1880's by wagon train, and settled near the Falk Store in the Payette valley. His father gave him a cayuse pony when he was six years old, along with a little red saddle and cowboy boots. He told Tom not to put too much time into learning to walk, as ponies were made to ride. When Tom died in 1970, following a colorful life of ranching, cowpunching, and hunting, he still had the saddle, though he'd outgrown the boots!

Below: Cayuse roundup, Middleton
Budding bronc rider
Bull-dogging, Nampa Stampede
Right: Women's liberation

From the days when the Shoshone first obtained horses from their kinsmen Comanches to the southwest, Idaho has been a horse country. Lewis and Clark could not have made it to the Pacific without horses bartered from the Shoshone — either to ride or eat. There is a lot of non-epicurean horse activity still going on in Idaho, built around special breeds like the Appaloosa, a lovely animal developed for its dappled beauty by the Nez Perce Indians. The wild mustangs are nearly gone, though a few still remain in the Lost River range and in the Owyhees. Horses are rarely essential to life in the West anymore, but are used mainly for recreational pursuits — pack animals, trail rides, rodeos — all reminders of an earlier and less hectic era. But people across the continent love rodeos, and Idaho has produced a few unique riders and ropers, including an all-girl rodeo at Mackay.

The tree-lined trout stream which meanders through the center of Idaho's capital city was called "La Riviére du Bois" by French trappers as early as 1812. From

that came the name of the fort at the river's junction with the Snake, and ultimately the name of the state's largest city. A century ago, before dams and pollution, salmon ascended the Boise River in such large numbers that travelers were kept awake at night by their splashing! The river was also an excellent source of beaver and a welcome oasis on the Oregon trail. With the shout of "Gold!" in 1862, the Boise Basin changed almost overnight. It triggered the establishment of a military post at the present townsite on the very day of the battle of Gettysburg, July 4, 1863. From that moment on, Boise grew — although not as the official capital without bitter battles with the settlers of Lewiston. Finally someone stole the state seal and spirited it to Boise in 1864. The Territorial Governor, Caleb Lyon, was supposed to have gone duck hunting, but he wound up in Boise, too! The same year Lyon executed a treaty with the Shoshone for possession of the Boise valley and all of the Owyhee country. No one knew how to established a price for the land so to this day no payment has ever been made.

By most standards Boise is a tiny capital city (population 78,500), but that suits Idahoans just fine. Basque sheepherders still graze their flocks and pitch their tents on the hills north of town, within a couple miles of the capitol dome. That is a comfort to Boiseans, and most of those to whom I have talked indicate they'd like to keep it that way.

The principal feature of the region and the determinant of its ultimate destiny will remain the mighty river which Bill Gulick so aptly described in his fine book, *Snake River Country,* as "born in incredible beauty . . . flowing through incredible isolation . . . nourishing incredible fertility . . . this is the Snake."

Today its waters continue to carve new canyons and roll the soil of a vast inland empire toward the sea.

> *"Dark brown is the river.*
> *Golden is the sand.*
> *It flows along forever,*
> *with trees on either hand."*
> — Robert Louis Stevenson

THE OWYHEE PLATEAU

There's a lot of room in this forgotten corner of Idaho. It's big sky country — a spacious land of sage, craggy buttes, wild bunch grasses, and surprising lava canyons. From the Raft River on the east and the Snake River on the north, clear to the Oregon border, it used to be all one county. Now it's three.

From the earliest times, the white man viewed these great southwestern uplands of Idaho as a terrifying wasteland — a gouged, eroded, scabrous desert. In 1836, Washington Irving described the area as "a place where no man permanently resides — a vast uninhabited solitude, with precipitous cliffs and yawning ravines, looking like the ruins of the world." Old-timers in a Silver City saloon might add, with convincing vehemence, that there are places where even the jackrabbits carry canteens!

Owyhee County alone is nearly 1,000 square miles larger than all of the islands of Hawaii. Unlike many other western names which have Indian roots, the mountains named "Owyhee" and the river to the southwest derive from an odd circumstance. Beginning in 1808 early traders, sailing around the Horn for the Columbia, often stopped at the Sandwich (Hawaiian) Islands for water, food, and refreshments of various sorts. The people living there called themselves by a word that the ship captains translated into English in their logs as "Owyhee." A number of "Owyhees" joined ships to the Columbia, and found their way up the Snake River with Donald MacKenzie, of the Northwest Fur Company, in 1818. They were skilled swimmers, good at diving under water to set beaver traps. Three Islanders, sent to search for beaver in the mountains and rivers to the south, never returned so MacKenzie named the range and the river in their memory. Later, missionaries to the Sandwich Islands changed the spelling to "Hawaii." At one time Fort Boise, at the mouth of the Boise River, was manned mostly by "Owyhees." There probably are less than 50 native Hawaiians now living in Idaho. This remote corner of the world is the only place where the initial phonetic spelling of their homeland remains.

Above: Jackrabbit
Right: Down Jordan Creek
toward South Mountain

The Owyhee Plateau is basically cattle and sheep country — a world of sparkling air, of vast unfenced ranges, of sagebrush, of native and introduced grasses, where the deer and the antelope still play. Livestock graze over steppes which once heard only the hoofbeats of the wild, including the bighorn sheep, the buffalo, the elk (which used to be a range animal until driven by man to the mountains), and the wild mustangs (of which 300 or so still roam the Owyhees). The cattle are mostly purebred these days, but some of them are descendants of the Texas longhorns, which 100 years ago were trailed nearly 2,000 miles to the Owyhee country to feed the miners. Cattlemen saw the potential of these rich grasslands and great ranches sprang up. A handful of remote spreads survives — green oases in the high valleys. At one time more cattle, sheep, and horses were trailed to the railhead and shipped from Murphy, now the county seat (pop. 75), than from any other point in the U.S. The original Owyhee cattle empire was a huge one, and as many as 100,000 longhorns ranged free during that era, helping to change the grasslands into sagebrush. Elliott's classic *History of Idaho Territory,* published in 1884, explained it succinctly: "The ranchers collected about them some stock, and while they slept their stock increased rapidly. Cattlemen, hearing of the excellent ranges for stock, drove cattle here in large numbers until today there are probably more in Owyhee County than in any other part of the Territory. The summer range for cattle is almost inexhaustible, every hillside furnishing a luxuriant growth of bunch grass."

Much of the Owyhee country was rolling grassland 150 years ago, not unlike the great plains of eastern Wyoming and Montana. There are still a few places where seas of grass ripple in the wind and you can hear Walt Whitman's voice echoing off the hills: "I believe a leaf of grass is no less than the journey work of the stars." Whitman called grass "the handkerchief of the Lord." A windburned stockman might not go that far, but he would agree that grass keeps the ranches going, just as in an earlier day.

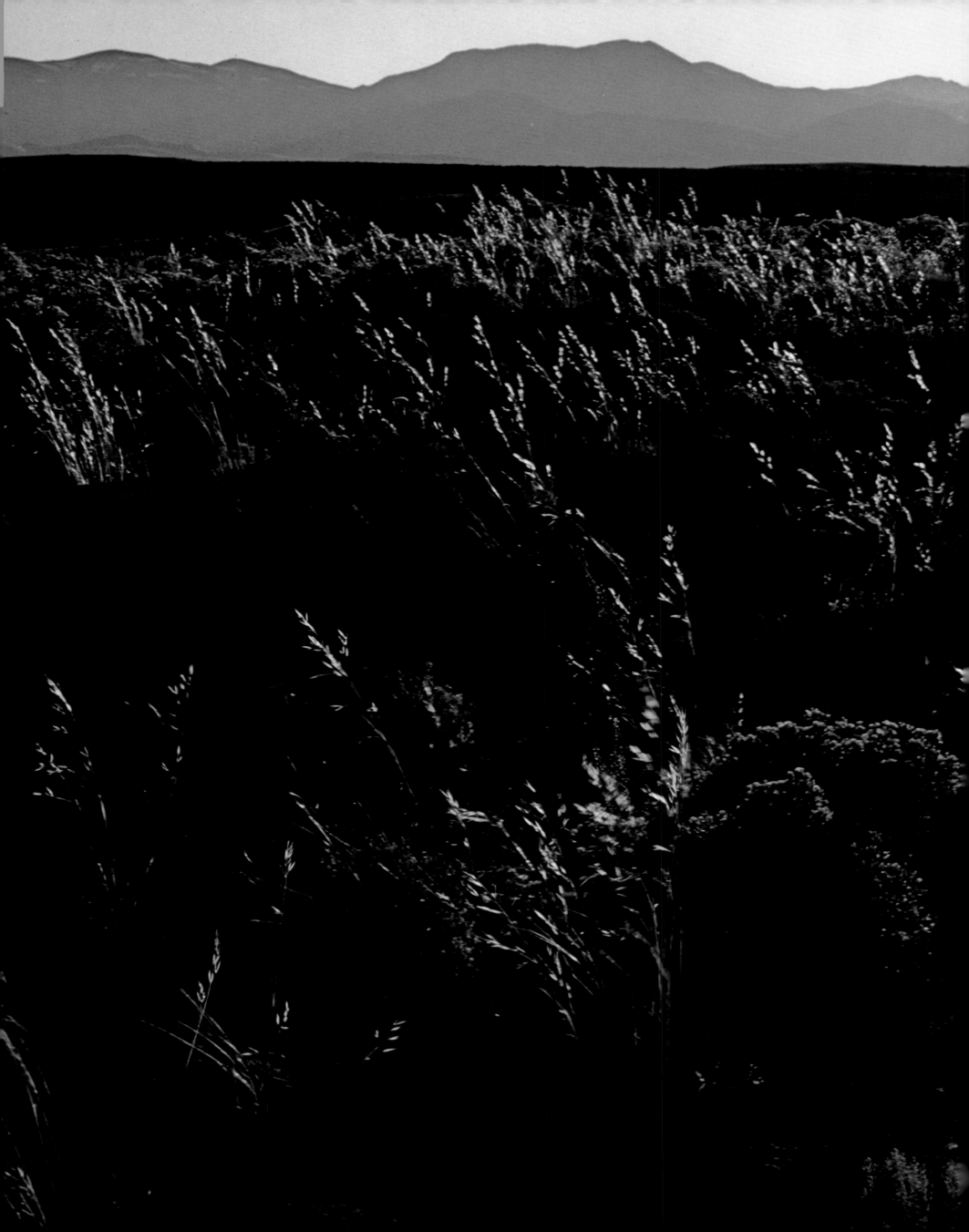

The grasses also attract the prairie dog, the gopher, the jackrabbit, and, in turn, their principal predator, the coyote — which gets some help from the badger and the hawk. Controversy still rages across the rangelands of the West over whether the coyote should be permitted to survive because it also kills calves and lambs on occasion; and people shoot badgers, eagles, and hawks, perhaps the best rodent-killers in nature, just for the fun of it. In my own travels of late, I have noticed a lot more coyotes and a lot fewer jackrabbits, which appear to be on the ebb tide of a cycle that repeats itself with regularity, no matter how much argument goes on. Everyone seems to agree on the rodents' ability to destroy rangeland when their populations are up. Whatever the truth, of one thing I'm certain: The major problem facing Idaho today is not coyotes, or badgers, but people.

If you get far enough into the backcountry, the Owyhee country is still old West, with its gun-toting, hard-riding cowboys, and its freedom from barbwire fences. Murphy boasts one big blowout a year, which brings in a few dozen ranch families from the outback and a scattering of rockhounds and city folk, interested in history. The principal attractions are beer, palaver, rock collections, beer, a historical museum, beer, demonstrations of how to find, cook, and prepare wild desert foods in the manner of early-day Indians, and beer. So far as settlement is concerned, however, Idaho's southwestern uplands remain sparse, visited only by stockmen, sportsmen, gem hunters, and an occasional prospector dreaming of another strike.

There was a time when silver and gold fever ruled Owyhee land. Gold was discovered on a wilderness creek by Michael Jordan in May, 1863. His find stimulated the age-old appetite for quick wealth from the ground. The hopeful rushed into the Owyhee plateau from all over the West. They stumbled across and developed one of the richest lodes of silver and gold in the world. All that is left of that amazing time are the ghostly towns, the crumbling buildings, weathered mine shafts, old cemeteries — reminiscent of a day

109

There were footprints upon the hill
And men lie buried under,
Tamers of earth and rivers.
They died at the end of labor,
Forgotten is the name.

when men and women, often ill-prepared, faced the elements, grew hungry, toiled with a desperate dedication, and developed callouses on their hands and their hearts. A few struck it rich, but many more barely scratched out a life. Those who survived walked tall, but their children often died in infancy. Each mining town and ranch settlement had its own cemetery nearby. Most of them have fallen into a state of neglect; cattle and sheep roam at will across the graves and scratch against the rail enclosures of the tombstones, many of which were made of wood. Coffins usually were made of crude lumber, covered with a thin black wool called challis, and lowered into the ground with a simple prayer or an old hymn. The epitaphs were classic, challenging the skills of the frontier poet and wood-carver:

> "John Bird, a laborer, lies here
> Who served the earth for sixty year.
> With spade and mattock, drill and plow;
> But never found it kind 'til now."

The winds echo a ghostly requiem through the ruins of these early settlements and cemeteries, and a balsam root flower set against a weathered mine building is all the "gold" that's left.

Queen of the mining towns was Silver City, 8,000 feet high on the slopes of War Eagle Mountain at the head of Jordan Creek — a citadel of hope for those who faced the overwhelming desolation of the Owyhees, where the heat of summer beat down cruelly and the snows of winter drifted deep enough to bury the town. At the turn of the century there were over 2,000 people living in this mountain fastness without railroad or auto — just horses, mules, guts, and a hunger for instant wealth. Nearly $70 million was extracted from its mines, and the gold and silver strikes which occurred here rivaled those of the famous Comstock lode of Nevada. The Orofino discovery near Silver City assayed at $7,000 a ton in silver and $8,000 a ton in gold. There were famous settlements like Flint, South Mountain, Happy Camp, Ruby City, Delamar, and

Booneville. In 1865 one digging called, in a hyperbole of understatement, the "Poorman Mine," produced a nugget of silver impregnated with gold and with ruby crystals which weighed 500 pounds and created a sensation at the 1866 Paris Exposition. It was a mine that for its richness transcended anything discovered to that time. The ordinary ore tailings of this mine assayed out at $5,000 a ton, justifying shipment across a continent and an ocean to Wales for special processing! While Silver City rivaled Virginia City, Nevada, as a producing area, it never quite reached that grandeur. With all that gold and silver around, however, a dynamite-proof safe, with someone to watch it, beat a baking powder tin under the floorboards of a cabin — *if* you could get your poke of nuggets or dust into town before being hijacked! Shortly after its beginnings in the back of a store in Boise in 1864, the state's banking system was pioneered in Silver City and in Idaho City, to the north, by Durell-Moore & Co. By 1867 it had become the First National Bank of Idaho.

In two years some 250 mining locations were recorded in the Owyhees. Prospectors searching for the truly legendary Blue Bucket Mine, never found, led to strikes all over Idaho. The legend stemmed from a party of immigrants who discovered gold nuggets in an Owyhee stream, hammered them out to use as sinkers for fishing, and marked the place with a blue bucket. Pretty high-class fishing gear! Everyone knows that miners and fishermen always tell the truth, and Sinker Creek survives in name today as testimony to the reputability of that legend. There are even a few prospectors still roaming the area, looking for the Blue Bucket lode! Most days a clear view of the Owyhee Mountains, including War Eagle and Florida peaks, and Cinnabar ridge connecting them, can be seen from Boise. It would be difficult to convince a few old-timers that Silver City will not again someday make the grass grow in the streets of the state capital!

Among other riches of Idaho, still bringing delight to their discoverers, are the semiprecious gem-minerals —and others not so precious—the thunder eggs, the

petrified woods, the jasper, and assorted quartz. Geologic history has made Idaho a gem-rich state, which attracts rockhounds to its remotest corners, including Owyhee County. John Beckwith says they are *never* carried away by their enthusiasm, and, like fishermen, their accounts of sources and quality of material discovered are *always* accurate. Opal tops the list in the Owyhees. The ancients believed that an opal brought good fortune to its owner. The Wangdoodle fire opals from Squaw Creek are named after a mythical bird of the area which is supposed to consort with the ubiquitous magpie. They are considered among the loveliest stones in the world. Important discoveries of this fascinating mineral were made in the Owyhees about 1893. Other principal locations for opals in Idaho are Spencer to the east, and the old Gem City area, north of Moscow. The North American Gem and Opal Company, operating from 1890 to 1904, recovered specimens as fine as anything found in Australia, the only other major opal-producing region of the world. Idaho opal is equal in color to anything known, although unstable for jewelry unless kept in liquid, set in chalcedony, or protected by a quartz cap.

Other treasures of the Owyhee country — unlike silver, gold, and opal, renewable ones — are the wildflowers, and the colorful desert lichens. Loveliest of these and quite unlike anything else in nature, is the sego lily, or "mariposa tulip," seen singly or in extensive displays. The white, yellowish-green, or lilac hues of their fluted petals can transform a dry desert hillside into a panorama of great beauty. The state flower of Utah, its sweet, nutritious bulb was an important food for the Mormon pioneers, as well as the Indians who preceded them. Best eaten in the fall, the root can be eaten raw, dried, baked, or roasted. It is a desert bounty which saved many a life when other food was scarce. There's a Japanese proverb that behind every flower stands God. The truth of this is never more evident than in the face of a delicate sego lily.

Other than old mines, a few fences, or a dim wagon

Left: Badger
Below: Chukar partridge
Antelope
Jack's Creek homestead

117

trail, remnants of man's mark on the Owyhees are few and far between. There's a crumbling stage station, or a weathered cabin here and there in some remote canyon, perhaps beside a trickling creek, like Jack's, where a man once figured he could scrabble a living from the soil, trap a little, and shoot enough game to survive. As far back as 1874, it was said that there was enough land on the south side of the Snake River in Owyhee County which, if properly irrigated, could support a million people. One hundred years later, that day still seems a long way off. For those of us refreshed by the wide open spaces, that's a happy thought.

Stories of abundance of game and fish in the "good old days" always strain my credulity a bit, but I like to believe. One apocryphal account appeared in 1882 in the Idaho Territory's first daily newspaper, the *Owyhee Avalanche,* still published weekly as the *Owyhee Nugget:* "Hon. T.D. Cahalan and Mr. Strode and family returned last Wednesday from a pleasure trip into the Mahogany Mountains in Owyhee County. They report having had a good time. Cahalan killed 45 deer in two days. He also killed 3 ibex (mountain sheep), 7 antelope, 147 grouse, 1 badger, and 1 snow rabbit. He killed 9 mallard ducks at one shot and 6 doves with another shot, and thinks a good hunter could kill 100 grouse (sage hens) in a day. He also caught 200 fish." No doubt Messrs. Cahalan and Strode and their miner friends ate well that month, but meat must have hung for quite a spell in the ice house — if they had one! There are still a lot of sage grouse in Owyhee County, and a relatively new bird, the chukar partridge, introduced from India in 1939. The chukar, now one of the prized upland game birds of the desert West, has thrived on the light brown cheat grass protected by rugged lava rock canyons like the one shown here.

Possibly the most rugged of these, said to be one of the deepest gorges for its width on earth, is Bruneau Canyon. It is reported that in its entire length of 67 miles there is only one place a horse can get down to water and only four places a man can descend. That fact may depend on how thirsty the man or the beast is

In any event, one can throw a stone across parts of the Bruneau Canyon that are 2,000 feet deep. It is breathtaking from the top looking down, the bottom looking up, or riding a kayak or rubber raft through its rapids. Floating the Bruneau (brown) River is a hazardous pastime, becoming more so because of the numbers and inexperience of the people who are trying it. There are current efforts to place the Bruneau under the protection of the national Wild and Scenic Rivers System. The proposal is not without controversy.

In keeping with the striking wildness of the Owyhees are its summer thunder and lightning storms. They strike a little terror into the hearts of the rangers and ranchers who know that so many of our range and forest fires are caused by dry lightning. These fireworks of nature are seldom accompanied by rain, but their flashing turbulence, lighting for seconds the high desert horizons, is unsurpassed. Like Mark Twain, many a wandering Owyhee cowpuncher could say, "I scratched my head with lightning and purred myself to sleep with the thunder." It's no accident that quite a few bucking broncs are named "Lightning," or that a favorite type of fiery liquid preferred by frontiersmen is often called "white lightning." Both have the same quality of surprise and stimulation.

Originally settled in Jordan Valley, just across the Idaho border to the west, the Basques of the Spanish and French Pyrenees have gradually immigrated to Idaho, forming the largest colony outside their homeland. About 10,000 of them have chosen the freedom and solitude of the Idaho mountains as their home away from home. A friendly, ruddy-cheeked people proud of their origins, the Basques have moved into many other fields besides stockraising, but their shepherds cling proudly to the ancestral occupation reflected in one of their songs:

"Far nobler in the mountains is he that
yokes the ox,
And equal to the monarch, the shepherd
of the flocks."

The Basque community holds a number of festivals each year. The Oinkari ("fast foot") dancers are famed throughout the world. Travel a mountain byway in the spring and you'll likely run across a band of sheep, a herder or two with their dogs and horses, and a canvas-covered wagon — their unique dwelling and nomadic trademark.

There is bitterness still between cattlemen and sheepmen over grazing rights on the public range — a fight for grass that began a hundred years ago as the herds and flocks grew larger. The shooting, if not the feeling, is over, and improved management is helping to restore the resource in places. The day may yet come when there will be enough grass for all, including even a few free-running wild mustangs.

One of the last Indian uprisings in Idaho occurred in the Owyhees when the Shoshone, Paiutes, and Bannocks banded together in the 1870's to terrorize the countryside. For years one of their leaders, Nampuh (Big Foot), from whom the town of Nampa gets its name, made life in the Snake River region memorable. He stood 6 feet 8½ inches tall and weighed 300 pounds, with a foot-span of 17½ inches! Seen in the mud beside a stream or along a ridge, his footprints struck terror into the heart of many a miner and rancher.

The Owyhee plateau doesn't look much different today from when Big Foot roamed it, or when the Indians hunted antelope or dug sego lily bulbs on its desert plateaus. The Duck Valley Indian Reservation, on the Idaho-Nevada border, boasts better fishing now, however, in Mountain View and Sheep Creek lakes.

Bisecting the county and the Reservation, the only paved highway to Nevada heads toward a seemingly limitless horizon. There are many square miles of unfenced range, where I have seen sage grouse on their booming grounds right beside the road, mule deer sneaking over a ridge, and wild eagles soaring. It should be quite awhile before the concentration of anything in the Owyhee country, except jackrabbits, gophers, or magpies, will exceed the human population of three-quarters of a person per square mile!

THE UPLAND EMPIRE

Stephen Vincent Benét could have been describing Idaho's great heartland when he wrote:

> *"Far north, far north are the sources of*
> *the great river,*
> *The headwaters, the cold lakes,*
> *By the little sweet-tasting brooks of the*
> *blond country,*
> *The country of snow and wheat,*
> *Or west among the black mountains, the*
> *glacial springs.*
> *Far North and West they lie and few*
> *come to them."*

It is an empire of grandeur and adventure that defies explanation and even the magic of the camera or the paintbrush. From the Snake River valley on the south to the Salmon River on the north, one is struck by the magnificence of its snow-mantled peaks, the wonder of its sculptured canyons, the enchantment of its broad valleys, the crystalline beauty of its lakes, its swift-flowing rivers, and its lazy meadow creeks.

These great uplands cover 25,000 square miles — 5,000 more than Switzerland, and scenically are every bit as spectacular. The region contains 10 major mountain ranges, 52 peaks over 10,000 feet in height — 6 of them over 12,000 feet — and the Continent's deepest gorge, the spectacular Hells Canyon, which at 7,900 feet is deeper by 2,600 feet than the Grand Canyon and, in places, 10 miles wide. It is a challenge not to sound too "boosterish" about it, but any description at all does require some adjectives.

Best known of its mountain ranges are the Saw-tooths, well-named for their jagged granite spires thrusting skyward. Several of Idaho's rivers have their trickling beginnings in its snowfields, including the famed Salmon and its Middle Fork. Less noted are the White Cloud Mountains to the east of the Stanley valley. Until they became the center of a molybdenum mining controversy in the late 1960's, dramatically influencing the course of Idaho politics, their beauty

was known only to a few backpackers and hunters.

Adding spice to the startling geography of the region is its colorful mining history. Beginning in the 1860's, these rugged mountains produced $100 million in gold and silver. They contain more ghost towns and mining camps than all the rest of the state put together.

The area is home to a variety of big game, including the elusive mountain lion, the bighorn sheep, the mountain goat, the lordly elk, and the black bear. It is, perhaps, the last land in the United States that contains such a variety of big game in such numbers, most of it in National Forests. The mountain lion is the most controversial, of course, because it kills elk and deer, often the older and less vigorous animals. Like all predators, it takes the most readily available food, including porcupines, pikas, grasshoppers, dead fish, and, on occasion, a band of domestic sheep. Two years ago the mountain lion joined the bear as a game animal in Idaho — a status of dubious safety, particularly with the advent of trailbikes and snowmobiles, which have made all backcountry wildlife highly vulnerable.

In 1972, following bitter battles among various interest groups, the extraordinary scenic and recreational qualities of these mountains were recognized by Congress, which established the Sawtooth National Recreation and Wilderness Area. There is current controversy over what to do with the Idaho Primitive area to the north — a 1.4-million-acre semiwilderness, which loses its Congressionally established primitive classification and protection in 1975.

A great deal of gold and an abundance of timber have come out of Idaho's upland empire since the 1870's. With careful management, timber harvesting, ranching, and mining can continue for many years to come, hopefully compatible with other more leisurely uses, now considered as valuable as lumber and beef, or silver and gold — in some places, even more so.

Left: Castle Peak (11,820 ft.)
Below: Miner's cabin in Ants Basin
below Patterson Peak (10,882 ft.)
"Grass widow," Squaw Creek
Castle Lake trail

Like for a couple of young fellows who decided that one of the best games of all was "getting ahold of pieces of country in your mind," learning to smell the mountains and their moods, deciding what grows there and why, how many steps climbing that peak would take, where this creek winds, and does that jewel of a mountain lake have any fish in it seems to them pretty important. Few would disagree that it's knowledge of value and that the best kind of ownership is to know these things from having been there one's self. In the process of getting there, you know yourself better, too.

Getting to the top of Mt. Hyndman (12,078) in the Pioneers; or Castle Peak (11,820) in the White Clouds; or Thompson Peak (10,776) in the Sawtooths, is kind of like that. En route there are some memorable sights and sounds and smells to experience, not the least of which might be the catching of an enameled golden trout, a rare high-altitude fish found in secluded mountain lakes — always difficult to reach, thank heaven! These fish lose their distinctive brilliance very quickly when removed from the water.

Almost as rare a sight these days is the otter, still seen along some of Idaho's backcountry streams. Four to five feet long at maturity, otters were last legally trapped in Idaho in 1971, when about 50 were taken. If you happen to camp at Otter Bar on the Middle Fork of the Salmon River, an otter will invariably steal a dozen eggs while you are asleep (so the guides will say). Under water an otter can easily capture the fastest fish that swims! When not hunting or traveling, otters like to build slides on clay banks and spend hours chuting into the water, apparently just for the fun of it. Maybe we ought to try it ourselves sometime!

The great mountain fastness of the Sawtooths, the Salmons, the Boulders, the Big Horn Crags, the Lost River Mountains, and a dozen other ranges, lies mostly over 5,000 feet with a lot of it approaching 10,000 feet. Geologists call this area the Idaho "batholith" (Greek for "deep stone"). It extends 300 miles north and south and 50 to 100 miles, east and west. These huge granitic upthrusts produced much of the mineral wealth of

Left: Sawtooth sound and silver
Below: Goat Creek beginnings
Redfish Lake creek
Otter on North Fork, Payette River

the state. Exposed by glaciers and snowmelt, they result in such a profusion of spectacular peaks and scintillating cataracts as to defy ordinary description. The infinitely fine spray against black rock in the cascade on page 132 reminds me of a 4th of July sparkler, or vice versa. My own experience tells me that the sound of running water is one of the most therapeutic in nature; and slaking one's thirst, belly-down, in a clear mountain stream comes as close as anything in my imagination to a drink from the fountain of eternal youth. We are often so intent on fishing or hurrying someplace that we seldom listen to the waters and hear their tale of power and beauty. In exploring Idaho's vast upland empire, I can't help but agree with Leonardo da Vinci, who wrote in 1512: "The eye, which is called the window to the soul, is the chief means whereby the understanding may most fully and abundantly appreciate the infinite works of nature; and the ear is second, inasmuch as it acquires its importance from the fact that it hears the things which the eye has seen." The mountains and waters of Idaho's heartland have much to appeal to both senses. It amuses many that Idaho is so widely known as the potato state, but perhaps it's to our benefit that outlanders continue to associate us dimly with Iowa and other such flat agricultural domains, rather than the great mountains, deep canyons, and sparkling streams which make up so much of our terrain.

The human re-creation possibilities in these relatively unspoiled mountain reaches make it easy to forget the treasure tales which began with the first group of prospectors to enter Stanley Basin 111 years ago. The granite spires and the crystalline lakes, like Toxaway, Pettit, Alturas, and Stanley; the unbelieveably sharp air, scented with pine and sage; the glacier lilies and mountain meadows carpeted with wildflowers — these are much the same; as is the light which varies moment by moment, and which, from dawn 'til dusk, enhances the beauty all about. Altogether they make for memorable experiences. Sunrise on Redfish Lake and the Sawtooths is an unforgettable sight.

But a good deal else is changing. Indeed, a new land rush is on from the Wood River Valley north to the Salmon. Most of the tiny villages seem unprepared for the onslaught of the developers, the trailbikers, the snowmobilers, the campers, the trailers, the hunters, et al, who, in turn, compete with the rancher, the miner, and the logger. There's big money in the "deuces wild" approach to the development of western land, paralleling in many ways the land rushes of the early-day homesteaders. A lot in the Wood River Valley or the Stanley Basin or on Payette Lakes can, with just a little imagination, be sold sight unseen to big city folk almost any day. Silver Creek has become a national mecca for campers and fishermen.

Dave Ketchum, attracted to the Wood River mines in 1879, built a cabin on the site of what is now a tourist village. He wouldn't be too surprised at the fancy saloons, nor the proposals to mine molybdenum in the Frog Lake basin of the White Clouds; but he might boggle a bit at the $75,000 condominiums springing up like prairie dog colonies all over the place. Many old-timers in the area disagree with the hoary axiom that this kind of growth is good. Even little Stanley (pop. 47 most of the year) is a boomtown in the summertime, attracting 12,000 people over a weekend! "Stompin' at Stanley" to a rock band on a Saturday night is the "in" way for tourists to mix with the natives. It's interesting how, after a full day's outdoor activity, people can stomp until the wee hours of dawn at 6,300 feet and tire less than in Los Angeles at sea level. Maybe it's the air! The proliferation of condominiums at so many Idaho resort areas is beginning to remind me of clusters of wood-stained rabbit warrens; but I guess people are as entitled to live in warrens as are rabbits, even though the latter have certain rights by prior settlement! In any event, most of them are *nice* warrens (the people ones, I mean); so, as Mary Hemingway says: "We still smile at the strangers."

Ernest Hemingway loved the tawny mountains of southcentral Idaho. He made Ketchum his home in the middle of them. In physical presence and literary

power his uniqueness reminds me of the great Idaho batholith to which he returned, in death, forever. A simple memorial beside Trail Creek, just north of Sun Valley, bears words he wrote about a friend who was killed in a duck hunting accident. These words became Papa's own epitaph and sum up the feeling about this part of Idaho for many of us:

> *"Best of all he loved the fall,*
> *The leaves yellow on the cottonwoods,*
> *Leaves floating on trout streams;*
> *And above the hills*
> *The high blue windless skies . . .*
> *Now he will be a part of them forever."*

Hemingway, who hunted the high Pahsimeroi country in the Lost River Range to the east of Sun Valley, was familiar with Copper Basin and Wild Horse Creek and the tiny mountain meadows, clipped close by grazing elk, with blue grouse thundering out of the thickets, and grass so lush that it makes the 18th green at Pebble Beach look like an asphalt parking lot. He understood the Idaho country and will always be identified with it, though strangely he never made it the setting for any of his writings.

Another famous writer wrote, in 1653, some words that remind me of the Wood River, its valley, and Silver Creek, which not only serves as the irrigation for lush hay meadows but also as one of the most noted "fluid envelopes" for trout in the world — a particular attraction for fly-fishermen. His name was Izaak Walton and his book, *The Compleat Angler,* is the most widely printed publication in the English language excepting the Bible. Said Walton: "When I would be content and increase my confidence in the power and wisdom of Almighty God, I will walk the meadow by some stream, and there contemplate the lilies that take no care, and those very many other little living creatures that are not only created but fed (man knows not how) by the God of nature. . . ."

One of the dividends of wading along Silver Creek or Wood River is the sight of a lovely marsh flower, or spotting one of the most handsome creatures to nest in Idaho, the American avocet. These cinnamon colored shore birds, spangled with white and black, march shoulder to shoulder up and down marshy shores, swinging upturned bills sideways, like farmers scything hay. In flight, they wheel through the air with drill-team precision, wintering as far south as Guatemala and summering north to Canada. A favored nesting place is Idaho's Bear River basin.

At the head of the Wood River Valley is the "queen mother" and oldest of all U.S. winter sports spas, Sun Valley. There are 26 other fine ski areas in Idaho, but because Averill Harriman's imagination and capital got there first, trying to build passenger rail traffic from the East, Sun Valley became, and with new management remains, the prototype of ski-resort America. Two hundred people attended its opening in 1936. Today at least 4,000 skiers a day swoop down the slopes of Mt. Baldy, and now and then Bing Crosby still sings "White Christmas" there for a national TV audience. Sonja Henie, though, has been replaced on the ice rink by Peggy Fleming.

In its heyday, between 1870 and 1890, the Wood River mines around Sun Valley and the hamlets that grew up to serve them — Bellevue, Hailey, Ketchum, Galena, Gimlet, et al — produced about $100 million in silver and gold. Resort development has attracted a lot more people and capital since, both here and in other places. Idahoans are particularly proud of their own corner of the state; like those who live and play in the northern lake country; or along the upper Salmon; or those who have a cabin on Cascade Reservoir, just east of Snowbank Mountain; or those who summer and winter on the Payette Lakes.

It likely would make little difference to Francois Payette, one of the most successful of the voyageurs who served in the fur trade of the Northwest. He first came to Idaho in 1818 with Donald McKenzie, of the Hudson's Bay Company (see THE EARLY DAYS), and his name remains on a pair of beautiful lakes and a lovely river, which he first explored. They are best

known to native Idahoans. Payette wound up as clerk in charge of affairs at Fort Boise, trading for beaver pelts and curing salmon from the Boise River for the other trading posts. He was described by a visitor as a "merry, fat, old gentleman of 50 who, although in the wilderness all the best years of his life, has retained that manner of benevolence in trifles, in his mode of dress, of seating you and serving you at table, of making you speak the French language 'parfaitment' whether you were able to do so or not, so strikingly agreeable in that mercurial people. During our visit we feasted with excellent bread, butter made from an American cow obtained from some missionary, baked, boiled, fried, and broiled salmon — all spiced with tales of his adventures in the wilderness." It is possible that tables set at the cottages and summer homes around the Payette Lakes today are a little fancier, but it is unlikely that the food or hospitality is any better than that of the portly French Canadian serving tea to the missionary wives and assorted adventurers visiting Fort Boise from 1836 to 1839. Big Payette Lake boasts not only colorful sailing regattas but also probably the most picturesque old sawmill in the state, with log booms making lovely patterns from the air.

Idaho's heartland from the Continental Divide to the Snake River, contains a diversity of wildlife unequaled in the western states — birds, big game, and many lesser creatures. Hunting, especially for big game, draws enthusiasts from all over the world. The state's Fish and Game Department does its best to manage the game populations and keep them in balance with their food supply and with man by a complicated permit system. Idaho's big game herds have become so well known that last year there were only three states — Mississippi, Maine, and New Hampshire — not represented among nonresident hunter licensees.

Certainly one of the rarest big game animals in Idaho's mountain wilderness is the Rocky Mountain goat. In spite of the fact that it dwells in remote, craggy, high country, its numbers are declining, due mainly to competition for forage and to the use of motorized

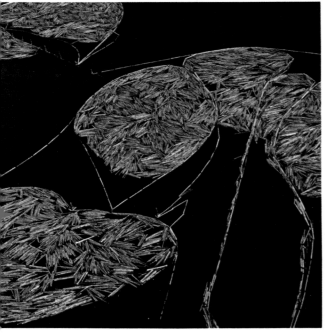

Below: Mount Borah (12,655 ft.)
Snowshoe rabbit trail
Right: Rocky Mountain goat

vehicles which give access to country heretofore very difficult to reach. While less graceful than the bighorn sheep, the goat's presence lends to many an otherwise gaunt and forbidding mountain top an aura of wildness and beauty. Living on glacier-carved escarpments, like those surrounding Shangri-la Lake in the Sawtooths, these remarkably surefooted animals survive on lichens, and, for days at a time, endure winter gales which roar about their cliffs and send snow banners streaming from the summits of the highest peaks. Their fleece has been compared to cashmere.

The valleys between these mountain ranges support a thriving cattle industry, with lush summer pasture in the mountain meadows and valley-grown hay for the hard winters. Del Clark, a cowpuncher for the San Felipé Ranch north of Mackay, says that the toughest job is riding out in 40° below zero weather in the Lost River valley below Mt. Borah (12,655 ft.) to cover up the cattle with snow to keep them from freezing to death. It's a tough way to earn a living, but looking at Del and hearing him talk about the mountains and the big game and the sunrises and the sunsets, you know he loves what he is doing and wouldn't trade it for any city job in the world at five times the income.

Few of the several hundred valleys in these great central uplands are over ten miles wide. The meandering streams which create them provide strips of arable land and pasture. One of the loveliest is Bear Valley or the headwaters of the Middle Fork of the Salmon, about 20 miles long by two miles wide and flat as a tabletop. As a grazing meadow, it is unsurpassed, and in scenic setting it is without equal in central Idaho.

The waters of Bear Creek are still gin clear and still serve the spawning Chinook. In 1844 the creek was described as "literally full of immense salmon from two to five feet in length." Bear Valley takes its name from the great number of bears that infested the area and the surrounding mountains at one time, probably feeding on salmon, much as they do in Alaska. In addition to its salmon runs, Bear Valley is also the location for a rare space-age metal alloy — something called

Left: Bear Valley Creek fishing bridge
Below: Moss-heather
A salmon returns to the river
Wild Spiraea

columbium-tantalum. Just as tantalizing is the scene at left of two Indians fishing off a bridge over Bear Valley Creek in the early mists. It is "a place where morning lies," and the end of a tedious journey from the Pacific Ocean for the giant salmon, which die upon completion of spawning. There are beauty and mystery even in the death and decay of this noble fish. We have learned how to land on the moon and to make soybeans taste like bacon, but we do not yet know by what magic all five species of Pacific salmon find their way back over unbelievably difficult obstacles to the very gravel bed where they were born from an egg the size of a pea. Few migrations in nature are as dramatic and few fish in history have provided as much food and sport for man as the Pacific salmon. They must be weary by the time they swim 1,000 miles to central Idaho, climbing ladders over eight dams, swimming through assorted pollution blocks and natural falls. It's a wonder they still come at all.

On their way from the sea, the salmon and the steelhead trout pass through the mile-deep canyon of the "River of No Return," and up many of its sparkling tributaries to spawn. Most famous of these is the Middle Fork, a whitewater pathway which rises at 7,000 feet in Bear Valley and falls to 3,900 feet at its confluence with the main Salmon, 150 miles to the north. Mountains rise on all sides to heights of 10,000 feet or more, creating incredible scenery and presenting travel requirements which most people never experience and few can even imagine. This rugged river and the surrounding country forced Lewis and Clark north to Lolo Pass and the Lochsa River in 1805 in order to find a way across Idaho. Rafting and kayaking both rivers have become popular sports, enjoyed by increasing numbers of people who find challenge in this country of tumbling rapids and excitement in the possibility of glimpsing a wild mountain sheep or cougar. Most of the important rapids are named and mapped. I have found it fun to measure their relative difficulty by the number of squirts of adrenaline experienced on the way through. Devil's Teeth rapids (over) is a relatively mild "4-squirter." Though the measurement is admittedly subjective, I've run 'em all the way up to 14!

The west slope cutthroat trout and its cousin, the rainbow, are found in the Middle Fork and dozens of tributary streams like Horse Creek or Chamberlain Creek. Fishing pressure has reduced their numbers, but it's still possible most anytime to catch a mess for breakfast to accent bacon, eggs, and flapjacks.

The region is one of the last strongholds of the cougar (mountain lion, panther, catamount), whose centuries-old reputation as a killer of game and livestock has brought it to the verge of extinction. There are many legends, both about the lions, and about the men who hunted them — like "Dead Shot" Reed of Emmett and "Cougar" Dave Lewis of the Salmon River Mountains. Lewis started out as an Indian fighter in the 1870's, switched to mountain lions about 1885, and by the time of his death in 1936, age 92, had killed at least 250 — lions, that is! Reed probably equaled his record. They didn't quite get them all, however.

The bighorn sheep, which also frequent the Salmon River and Hells Canyon country, gave rise to the name of the "Sheepeater" Indians who lived there and became skilled at pursuing and capturing them for food. The Sheepeater "war" of 1879 was a classic mountain skirmish in which the brutal terrain forced the U.S. Cavalry and the Indians into a standoff.

A bighorn ram can weigh 350 pounds. Old mountain men swear that instead of clambering down toilsomely over broken rocks, the bighorns make an easy job of it by leaping headlong over precipices 50, yes, even 100 feet high, alighting headfirst on their horns, which are strong enough to be unbroken by the shock and elastic enough to throw them 10 to 15 feet into the air — the next time alighting on all four feet! That *could* be a tale out of a Placerville saloon, but having seen bighorn rams butting heads in battle during mating season, I'm inclined to believe it, though I'd sure like to see it.

What to do with a part of the home of the sheep and the lion, the magnificent Hells Canyon of the Snake River, has become a major controversy. In 1834, Captain Benjamin Bonneville, who was the first to explore this deepest of all gorges in North America, wrote: "The grandeur and originality of the views presented on every side, begger both the pencil and the pen. Nothing we have ever gazed upon in any other region could for a moment compare in wild majesty and impressive sternness with the series of scenes which here at every turn astonish our senses and fill us with awe and delight."

Once again, the conflict is between our need and hunger for energy and our need and hunger for the tonic of wildness. The battle lines are already clearly drawn over the last 125 miles of free-flowing water on the Middle Snake, which includes Hells Canyon. Elsewhere, the Columbia and Snake Rivers are virtually one big reservoir from Portland, Oregon, to Lewiston, Idaho. The basic question remains: How many more wild canyons need we destroy to gain the energy; or what are we willing to give up instead? We must ask the question seriously, because there is no

returning. A canyon buried beneath a reservoir is a canyon gone forever. It's easy to measure the dollar value of a kilowatt; not so of a wild canyon. It is an agonizing choice with no universal solution.

The Seven Devils Mountains are keeping a watchful eye on the outcome. They form the eastern skyline of Hells Canyon for 40 miles. He Devil Peak is the highest, at 9,393 feet, 7,900 feet above the river's surface. These mountains proved to contain the earliest copper strike in Idaho discovered in 1862. The Peacock mine was named for the robin's egg or peacock blue color of some of the large ore veins protruding from the ground which turned out to be over 20 per cent pure copper. In spite of the tough terrain, the ore was sacked, tied on mules, packed seven miles over the ridge to Bear Creek, and thence shipped to the big Anaconda smelter in what is now Montana. Kleinschmidt Grade into Hells Canyon, built to carry the ore down to river steamers, is named for one of the eastern investors in that mine. The tiny mountain village of Cuprum (Latin for "copper") is now a departure point for backpackers and trail riders. To date, the Seven Devils mines have produced far less than the initial investment in them, so the country remains principally an outdoor recreation and timber land.

Of all the mining in this mountain empire, perhaps the best known was the Boise Basin, with Idaho City as its focus, and places like Placerville, Quartzburg, Thunder Mountain, and Boston Bar writing its history. By 1863, sixteen thousand people had rushed into the Basin and settled in camps all over the place. Mines at remote log cabin settlements like Boulder, north of Ketchum, sprang up at elevations of 10,000 feet, and delivered up over a million dollars in gold and silver to those hardy enough to stand the brutal winters and relative inaccessibility. Boulder's remains are still there, in one of the loveliest mountain basins in Idaho.

An early writer from California visited the area in its heyday and reported that "Politicians from all parts are daily arriving. Experience has proved that as a class their presence permeates the very atmosphere they

Below: Wild columbine
Boulder Basin ghost town
20th Century Mine, Stibnite
Right: Pioneer cemetery, Idaho City

breathe. Idaho, as a virgin territory, rich beyond all imagination in mineral treasures and as yet unencumbered with the curse of local debt, offers a rich harvest. Ere another year passes by, we shall have an Augean stable which even Hercules cannot cleanse. Lawyers and doctors are arriving in overwhelming numbers and, with some bright exceptions, they are composed of ignorant quacks and foc'sle shysters. Woe to the man who takes either their pills or their advice! There is no jail in Idaho City, but plenty of rope and trees!"   Outside capital from the East developed many of the mines, like Thunder Mountain (Pittsburg), and the 20th Century Mine near Stibnite (South Dakota). A famous mining camp, Roosevelt, was buried beneath the waters of Monumental Creek when a landslide dammed it up. It's likely the only ghost town in the West you have to explore with scuba gear!

A Sunday in Idaho City, when most of the miners took the day off, was described: "The thermometer stands at 92° in the shade — rotgut 25 cents — myriads of bottleflies pregnant with poison sailing through the air — whiskey the beverage, and monte the game — angels weep, men curse, dogs fight, and heavy peals the thunder from the surcharged atmosphere, announcing the displeasure of the Supreme. Rapine and murder are in our midst; a breathless corpse lies weltering in his blood, with a knife penetrated from breast to abdomen. The Sabbath closes with a clouded moon. Reader, dost thou like the picture? 'Tis but a fraction of the truth of a Sunday in Boise Basin."

All debts, feuds, and kisses were settled weekly in the mining camps, and the man who neglected to pay his butcher, apologize for quarreling with his friend, or forgot to visit his lady love was forever dishonored. With 33 whiskey shops in full blast in Idaho City alone, and alcohol mixed with juniper berries selling at 10 cents per gallon, it's no wonder that the pioneer cemeteries filled up at a pretty fast rate. The trees seem to grow faster and taller around those old cemeteries than anyplace else in the upland empire. I've often wondered why!

IN MEMORY
OF
BLANCHE ALEXANDER
WHO DEPARTED THIS LIFE
JUNE 7th 1864
NATIVE OF LOUISIANA
AGED 54 YEARS

Left: Heart of the Monster
Below: Palouse pictograph
Appaloosa scratch
Nez Perce matriarch

THE NEZ PERCE COUNTRY

For six or seven thousand years, a loose confederation of Indian bands, who wore shell ornaments through pierced noses, dominated an area of what is now Idaho from the Salmon River on the south, through the Clearwater country, to the Coeur d'Alenes on the north. The Nez Perce, like many tribes, identified themselves with the natural features of their environment — the stupendous mountain ranges, the vast forested highlands, the rugged canyons, and silver threads of rushing streams running through them. They believed that the Earth was their mother, who nourished them with the bounty of her land and her waters, and they lived in harmony with their surroundings. They were brothers to the animals and to the trees and to the grasses and the rain. They raised wild golden eagles for the black and white tail feathers and to trade with other tribes for horses. Many of their legends came from these associations.

On the banks of the Clearwater River near Kamiah stands a volcanic outcropping which the Nez Perce say is the "place of beginning." Its-welx was a huge monster that swallowed all animal beings and imprisoned them in his stomach. Coyote, a legendary hero, permitted himself to be swallowed by the monster, and killed it by cutting out its heart which he left on the ground near the river where you can still see it. He then carved up pieces of the monster's body, casting them in all directions to form the various tribes of man. He finished by shaking the blood from his fingertips onto the ground, saying, "Here I make the noble Nee-Me-Poo (Nez Perce) tribe, few in number, but strong and pure." These qualities are mirrored in the face of matriarch Elizabeth Wilson who died in 1973, age 91.

The uniquely marked and sturdy "Palousey," or Appaloosa horse, was ridden by the Nez Perce and often called the buffalo horse. It is one of the oldest breeds known. A few were brought to the New World by the Spaniards and scattered throughout the West, but it is

to the Nez Perce living along the Palouse River that the breed owes its modern name, and to them goes the credit for perpetuating it. The Indian rode these animals to the Great Plains to hunt buffalo. Today a one-lane dirt road follows that trail for 120 miles across central Idaho, through the Magruder Corridor between the Salmon River Breaks and the Selway-Bitterroot primitive areas. It crosses the Bitterroot Mountains into Montana at 6,600 feet and has been called by a number of early surveyors, geologists, and cavalrymen "the most terrible trail on all the Continent of North America." I asked Gomer Lemon, a modern mountain man searching for a lost horse along the Nez Perce trail last September, what he thought about the country. "Man, it's just like riding through ghost country," he answered. "But you get a-hunting out there for an hour in these damn hills, and you are at peace with the world. You have no worries — nothing."

Gomer's link to those timbered mountains was like that of the Nez Perce — very personal. I'm sure he had his own "Wey-ya-kin," or guardian spirit, which the Indians sought from youth by isolated fasting and meditation in the mountains. Traveling that trail during fall's first snowfall, I felt the spirits everywhere, and on a misty morning photographed what might have been one in the silhouette of a burnt pine snag.

The green lands of north Idaho are made up largely of white pine, spruce, larch, and red cedar. Idaho is fifth in the nation in the volume of standing saw timber. Over 30 per cent of the state's 54 million acres are forested, most of it in federal ownership. The world's largest white pine is near Elk River — 219 feet tall, with a diameter of 6 feet 8 inches. When Lewis and Clark followed the Lolo Trail through these quiet virgin forests, they found little game. In fact, they nearly starved to death and had to eat some of their horses, and even candles, to survive. Fire and logging have created sunlit openings in which grow the grasses, the berries, and the browse that have made the Clearwater country a haven for a variety of wildlife, including the largest herd of elk left in the state. Following logging

Below: Pine logging, Clearwater country
Backcountry bobcat
Idaho White Pine, state tree
Right: Bunchberry (ground dogwood)

or fire, grasses, willow, bitter cherry, bunchberry (ground dogwood), thimbleberry, and others move in — food for a diversity of birds and mammals that do not exist in old virgin forests. So, in their place and thoughtfully controlled, fire and logging can add much to the attraction of these mountains. All we really need is the insight to recognize, as did the Indians, that Mother Nature is boundless in her bounty if we treat her with respect, feeling, and perhaps even just some plain old common courtesy.

The Lolo Trail is a rugged trace ("Lolo" is Chinook Indian jargon for "carry"). Even the explorers' experienced Indian guide had difficulty finding and staying on it. The trail follows the ridge tops above the Lochsa River. Beside the trail is a fine example of western red cedar in the Bernard Devoto Memorial Grove. Devoto was a distinguished author who spent much time editing the journals of Lewis and Clark for popular reading. He often camped at the spot. At his request, his ashes were scattered, upon his death in 1955, amongst

Left: Devoto Memorial Cedar Grove

Below: Raccoon

Pack string crossing Selway River

Bull elk, Clearwater country

the trees he loved so well. The largest single tree in Idaho is a cedar, named for former Governor and Senator Len Jordan. Near Goat Mountain in the Clearwater country, it is 133 feet tall and 16½ feet in diameter.

The explorers' report of the trail discouraged its use for many years thereafter, and it was left pretty much to the Indians. Chief Joseph and his harassed band followed it in their historic trek toward freedom in Canada in 1877. They never made it. Joseph's surrender speech, pretty much ending the Indian "wars" in the West, concluded with the unforgettable words: "Hear me my chiefs. I am tired; my heart is sick and sad. From where the sun now stands, I will fight no more forever." The Nez Perce started with some 10 million acres in Washington and Idaho. A 750,000-acre reservation remains, and in 1965 Congress established the Nez Perce National Historical Park, consisting of 23 separate sites over a 12,000 square mile area surrounding the Reservation east of Lewiston.

Not far out of Clarkia, in Latah County, is a pretty little
stream in the deep forest called Emerald Creek. Wood
ducks and harlequin ducks can occasionally be seen
drifting through its shaded pools. A unique and charm-
ing wildflower, the evening primrose (named *Clarkia
pulchella* after Captain William Clark, who first discovered them along the Clearwater River) is also found
in the shady mountain canyons all about. The flowers
are the airiest blossoms one can imagine, and are
often called by the common name of "pink fairies."

But it is not for such beauty that this tiny stream is
world famous. Rather, it is for garnets. The east fork of
Emerald Creek is the principal source of the star garnet, found elsewhere in the world only in India. This
unique, plum-colored gemstone, with 4 to 6 rays, is
rarer than the star ruby or star sapphire. It became
Idaho's state stone in 1967, and gem hunters from all
over the world travel to Emerald Creek, don hip boots,
and with a screen, box, and bucket, probe and sift its
waters for this precious jewel. The translucent stones
at left are of a different variety of garnet, tumble-
polished to bring out their beauty. A natural almandite
garnet crystal, with a 6-rayed star cabachon cut from it,
is hand-held at right.

Emerald Creek runs into the Potlatch River, a name
derived from an ancient Indian festival of gift-giving.
The Potlatch enters the Clearwater above Lewiston,
which, with its sister city, Clarkston, across the river in
Washington, memorializes the passing of the explorers through this area. The Clearwater joins the Snake at
Lewiston — at 739 feet, the lowest elevation in the state
— and is a highway for some of the largest salmon and
steelhead to come into Idaho. From the summit of the
mountain rim to the north, 2,000 feet above town, one
can view the vast rolling hills of Washington's part of
the Palouse country to the west, as well as the junction
of the two rivers. Irvin Cobb declared it to be the most
breathtaking vista of his entire journey through the
Northwest.

Like the trout, salmon, and steelhead, many of the
rushing mountain streams of Idaho are home to a de-

lightful little bird, the water ouzel, or dipper, that not only walks under water but also opens its wings and "flies" underwater too. Its habit of bobbing up and down as it flits from rock to rock has given it the colloquial name of "teeter-ass." It feeds on insect larvae on the rocks, nests behind waterfalls, and sings deliciously year around.

Mother Nature must have had something special in mind for the Nez Perce peoples and those who followed, for, in addition to giving it forested mountains and rushing waters to the east, she blessed the western part of this region with a blanket of thick loam around Lewiston and Moscow, in places over 100 feet in depth, that grows some of the richest grain and vegetable crops in the nation. Named by the French trappers, the Palouse ("waving grass") country because of the vast tablelands of wild bunch grass that grew there, it was a grazing land for wild game and a great attraction to the white settler. The hills of the Palouse have a charm for all who see them in their glory of grain and hay fields — "the land that lies 'neath the summer skies, in the heart of the happy hills."

Moscow was originally called Paradise City. The agriculturally rich valley roundabout still bears that name. In addition to wheat and other grains, it produces peas, alfalfa, and a variety of fruits and vegetables, which originally were shipped by wagon to Lewiston and then by stern-wheeler to western markets. There seem to be many stories about how Moscow got its name — from that of a settler who named it for a town near his home in Pennsylvania, to that of a Russian immigrant with the improbable name of Hogg!

Whatever the case, up to 20 years ago the area around Moscow and Lewiston was the best pheasant country in the state, producing as many as 2,000 birds per square mile. The small homestead farms provided ample cover and feed for these colorful game birds, when originally introduced. The advent of large-scale industrial farming has pretty much eliminated their roosting and nesting cover here and in other parts of Idaho.

Discovery of gold on Orofino Creek in 1860 (see THE EARLY DAYS) was responsible, in the end, for the Nez Perce "war." The original treaty in 1859 reserved almost all of their traditional homelands to the Nez Perce, including their treasured camas prairies; but it was doomed to failure when gold was discovered within the Reservation boundaries. The white miners simply would not stay off. Over 10,000 of them moved into the Clearwater country after Pierce's strike. The result was predictable. Indian bands, like those under Chiefs Whitebird and Joseph, harassed miners and settlers along the Clearwater and Salmon Rivers. In a pitched battle in 1877 at what is now Whitebird Hill, the Indians killed about 35 U.S. Cavalrymen without a loss themselves. This led to General Howard's pursuit of the non-treaty Nez Perce across 1,500 miles of some of the most rugged country left in America. It ended with Joseph's surrender in Montana. With the Indians settled down, the farmers went to work in earnest on the rich Palouse country. In 1875, a Spokane newswriter

said of the area around Kamiah: "The Nez Perce prairi
is in a most flourishing condition, and the farmers c
that district are rapidly gaining wealth. I know of on
man who came into the country six years ago wit
nothing but four broken down cayuses. Last fall he sol
16,000 bushels of flax for 98¢ a bushel! When I firs
arrived, I had only enough to build a house costin
$475.00. I now have a standing offer of $6,000.00 fc
my farm." What would that farm be worth today?

Pioneering the Nez Perce country is not over. I
response to an inquiry about her photo, Mary Simeone
milking the goat at left, sent me the following lette
postmarked Elk River:

"My husband, Herb, and I arrived with our tw
daughters in April, 1972, prepared to pitch our tent o
our 40 acres of uninhabited land 4 miles north of here
We came from the smog and filth of New York City i
search of a better life. I am a former teacher, my hus
band, a former Air Force pilot.

"In our enthusiasm and naiveté, we thought we coul
begin clearing our land and build immediately, but E
River's severe winters had left 5 feet of snow still on th
ground, even in April. Finally, in June, we set up a ten
and an old wood cook stove, given to us by a loc
farmer. I started housekeeping under a big fir tree, an
Herb started building an A-frame barn. He had nev
built anything before in his life! We accumulate
chickens, a pig, and 3 goats. I delivered a healthy sc
by natural childbirth and brought him home to our ten
where we continued to live until October. We the
moved into our house, built mostly of logs, which Her
had cut, peeled, and raised by hand with the help
many new friends made in our short stay in Idaho.

"We consider ourselves native Idahoans now. W
love our land, the beautiful view of the mountains, th
birds that visit us, the clean air, the fresh water, hikin
to town all winter by snowshoe, teaching our childre
at home. We also love our freedom."

As David Grayson said, "No country, after all, pro
duces any better crop than its inhabitants."

Left: Cave Lake from Rainey Hill
Below: White-tailed deer, Blue Lake
Lily pad patterns, Black Lake
Beauty Bay, Lake Coeur d'Alene

THE NORTHERN LAKELAND

The 8,000 square miles of Idaho's northernmost re
gion are rich in natural beauty and mineral wealth. This
lovely corridor between Washington and Montana is a
succession of sparkling lakes and rounded mountains
timbered to the top. In summer it is quite different in
appearance from much of Idaho's craggy heartland
which has high peaks above timberline that retain
snow the year around.

There are hundreds of lakes scattered throughou
the region, the most famous being Pend d'Oreille
Coeur d'Alene, and Priest. These three combined have
a water surface of 150,000 acres. Pend d'Oreille is one
of the largest fresh water lakes in the U.S. Like so many
places in Idaho, it was named by the French trapper
after Indians who lived in the region who wore orna
ments hanging from their ear lobes. The same is true of
the Coeur d'Alenes ("Pointed Hearts"), who were
thought of by the mountain men as shrewd and some
what tricky traders.

A Shoshone County pioneer, writing about the north
country in 1903, described it as a land of "innumerable
sparkling streams of the purest water, alive with sal
mon and trout; also affording the one indispensable
requisite to profitable mining . . . and with dense tim
berlands which will, when amply developed, be a
source of great wealth." His excitement about the min
ing and timber prospects was only exceeded by his
enthusiasm for the various forms of wildlife found in the
area — bear, moose, deer, cougar, lynx, bobcat, blue
grouse, and ptarmigan. They are still there, and even a
small band of caribou still drifts through the mountains
above Priest Lake each year. The panhandle also has
probably the largest herd of the shy and elusive white
tailed deer in the state.

Besides the large and famous lakes, there are
numerous smaller ones. Their presence makes every
bend in the road a new adventure. Typical is a group of
nine strung along the lower Coeur d'Alene River, each

up to two miles in diameter, shallow, attracting a variety of waterfowl and shore birds. They are, like Cave Lake seen from Rainey Hill, wet jewels in an emerald empire of green forests.

Several of north Idaho's lakes and lovely rivers are facing bio-strangulation from sewage and mining pollution, however. Early action is necessary to keep these pristine waters from turning into cesspools. We need not lose this beauty as have so many other states. For it's the kind of value that has provided more people from all over the world with an appreciation of our outdoor wealth than anything else — boys, girls, their adult leaders and parents from 47 countries and every state in the Union. The attraction has centered on the shores of Lake Pend d'Oreille at Farragut. A naval training center during World War II, this lovely peninsula was later made into a state park. In 1965, it was the site for the National Girl Scout Roundup. Since then it has hosted a World Scout Jamboree and two U.S. National Boy Scout Jamborees. These thousands take home with them impressions of Idaho, its people, its environment, and the way we treat it. Some of *them* don't treat it too well, either. Perhaps it's not too late for us to learn together.

The waters of Pend d'Oreille are famous as well for mighty Kamloops (rainbow) trout, which push 40 lbs. in weight. The deep green woodland around the lake provides homes for an intriguing variety of birds and animals — and children — and people in little villages on the timbered terraces, like Clark Fork, Kootenai, and Hope — the last almost prophetic, through its name, about the future of north Idaho.

I'm reminded of the poem by Grace Crowell:

"I shall keep some cool green memory in
*   my heart . . .*
It may be this green remembered tree
That I shall turn to if the nights be long,
High on a hill, its cool boughs lifting free,
And from its tip, a wild bird's joyous song.
A weary city dweller to survive
Must keep some cool green memory alive."

Left: Outfall of Harrison Lake
Below: Priest River moods
St. Maries River joins the St. Joe
Copeland ferry crosses the Kootenai

That cool green memory includes, of course, the forested Selkirk Mountains, which bisect Idaho's northland and contain some of the loveliest high lakes in the West. Many of these are still uncharted, unnamed, and seldom seen. Certainly 30-acre Harrison Lake and the unusual stair-stepping falls flowing from it at left, would qualify. Eight miles to the west lies a 46-mile-long deep blue water lake, named for an early missionary. "Kaniksu," naming the National Forest around the lake, is an Indian word meaning "black robe." Priest and Upper Priest Lakes are famed for giant Mackinaw (lake trout), running up to 55 lbs. The Priest River leaves the lower lake to join the Clark Fork. Like the "shadowy" St. Joe, the lovely St. Maries and Coeur d'Alene rivers to the south, and the Kootenai which slants briefly through northeastern Idaho via Bonners Ferry en route to Canada, the Priest River has many moods. Watching these rivers and lakes as the sun goes down, one wonders, with Hugh Prather, how there can be pettiness and sunsets on the same planet.

Below: Coeur d'Alene River
Cataldo Mission
Priest Lake derelict
Right: Priest Lake sunset

Left: Falls on Copper Creek
Below: State flower, the syringa
Idaho grizzly bears
Bull moose — a singular party!

These water "highways" served trappers and settlers in the early days — loggers, fishermen, and boating enthusiasts, today. Years ago, the old wood-fired steamboat, *Tyee,* was used to tow booms of logs down Priest Lake to the river, whence they were floated to the sawmills.

Equally renowned in early transportation efforts was the historic Mullan Road, built between 1859 and 1862 to connect Fort Benton on the Missouri River with Walla Walla on the Columbia — sort of a "Northwest Passage" between waterways. Under incredibly trying conditions, including 26 bridge crossings of the Coeur d'Alene River and 46 crossings of other streams, Captain Mullan finally finished the job, passing through the famous Coeur d'Alene mining camps of Wallace, Kellogg, and others. He often stopped at the Cataldo Mission house, originally established in 1848 to serve the Coeur d'Alene Indians.

The mines of the Coeur d'Alene district are the richest in Idaho, producing so far nearly $2 billion — at least four times the value of silver dug from the Comstock Lode of Nevada. They still produce 10 per cent of the world's total silver and 50 per cent of the silver dug in the U.S. Silver was discovered in north Idaho in 1884, when Noah Kellogg left his jackass to browse while he poked around the area looking for a way to get rich. When he returned, the burro was grazing on top of an exposed outcropping of ore, which became, in time, the Bunker Hill and Sullivan mine. Kellogg died penniless. So did his jackass. But they are remembered in the name of a town and of a skiers' mountain, the name of which was recently sterilized from Jackass to "Silver Horn" Ski Bowl.

With silver the king and no copper strikes known in north Idaho, it's odd that there are a lovely stream and falls about five miles south of the Canadian Border which bear the name. On the forested banks of Copper Creek, a small tributary of the Moyie River, a visitor might spot the Idaho state flower — four snowy white petals with a "heart" of gold, the syringa. This shrubby variety of the mock orange, three to ten feet high, was

first described by Meriwether Lewis who no doubt smoked peace pipes made from its tough wood by the Indians. The Indians also used syringa to make bows and wicker cradles for their babies and soap from its crushed leaves.

The Copper Creek area is also moose country. About 100 are harvested by permit in Idaho each year. It's grizzly bear country, too, but the scattered few along the Canadian Border, and also near Yellowstone, are protected. The Indians and the settlers found the moose a good meat source. It was often the other way around with the grizzlies! Perhaps that's why the bears appear doomed to extinction. From the days of the earliest explorers, grizzly bears have borne the undisputed title of America's fiercest and most dangerous big game. Having little fear of primitive Indian weapons, grizzlies were at one time indifferent to the presence of man. There was no higher badge of courage or prowess to be worn by a warrior than a necklace of grizzly claws.

Winter in the northern mountains is cold and the snows are deep, but not enough to discourage the skier at Schweitzer Basin or the dogsledders or the trappers who still run winter lines for mink, marten, ermine, and beaver. It is a serene time when the earth goes to sleep under the snow. Not only the furbearing predators but also the snowshoe hare, the junco, the Canada jay, the chickadee, the grouse, and many others bring life to the quiet forest. Ski-touring is bringing back to many people an appreciation of winter in the woods. Snowmobiles get there, too, of course, but with such a clatter that they cannot possibly see and hear the life that is frightened out of the area ahead of them.

On the west side of Priest Lake, at Nordman, the annual Northwest sled dog championships are held, harking back to a pre-snowmobile day, when dog sleds were the fastest way to get around the backcountry from November to April or later. This is just one more example of the variety of life-style in Idaho's north country — a sparsely populated land where the song of

Below: Rocky Mtn. (Canada) Jay
Moyie River music in Purcell Mts.
St. Joe River portrait for water people
Right: Spring maple — a promise of renewal

the mountains is carried by a thousand tumbling streams, and the spirit of the early people who inhabited the country is mirrored in a quiet river. Indeed, the word Kootenai is a corruption of the north Idaho Indians' own name for themselves, "Kutenai," which means "water people."

When winter writes its message in shivers on the drifting snows, we dream of the green beginnings of another spring — the promise of renewal in the changing seasons and landscapes and people. This feeling is well expressed in a paraphrase of the poet:

"If on this night of still white cold
I can remember May
New green of trees and underbrush
The scent of earth, and noon's blue hush.
If on this night of bitter frost
I know such things can be,
I shall believe the tales men tell
Of columbine and asphodel,
And immortality."

194

IDAHO TEXTURES

From afar the textures of Idaho can be as intriguing as close up. The U.S. Geological Survey decided to have a look from 567 miles, setting up the Earth Resources Observation System (EROS). Whether there is any relationship between that acronym and the fact that Eros was the son of Aphrodite, goddess of love, I'm not sure. Hopefully, it means we are learning to use our technical skill to understand and appreciate a little better this "spaceship" on which we all live. The Earth Resources Technology Satellite I, takes a new photo of the same area every 18 days. It is giving scientists a new tool with which more wisely to plan the use of our planet's natural resources.

A section of north Idaho, including Coeur d'Alene Lake and River; part of Lake Pend d'Oreille (top); the Palouse country (lower left); and the Clearwater and Bitterroot Mountains (midright) is shown on the facing page. In this infrared image, healthy vegetation appears red; clear water, black; silty water, blue; clouds and snow, white; cultivated fields, light yellowish; and cities, grey-blue. Focusing down within this vast overlook, is a closeup of one of nature's "paintings" — lichens on a rock, similar in texture and color, proving Marjorie Mighell's point that Nature is the master decorator, from whatever distance we view her works.

Few of us will ever view the earth from a spaceship, but there is exhilarating beauty close by if we take the time to look. And so, we conclude this book with a brief look at things frequently passed by, from floral and lichen patterns, to leaf patterns, to wood grains, to the "deep white fur" of glittering snow. Colors seldom clash outdoors, for the light has a quality that blends natural loveliness, whatever the hues. Even the works of man, weather and time-stained, also take on a complementary beauty.

This, then, is Idaho — large and small. However we view it, there is a bit of the unknown somewhere. Go and discover it.

Above: Lichen close-up

Right: Satellite view, North Idaho

2

3

5

6

7

8

9

10

11

12

13
200

14

15

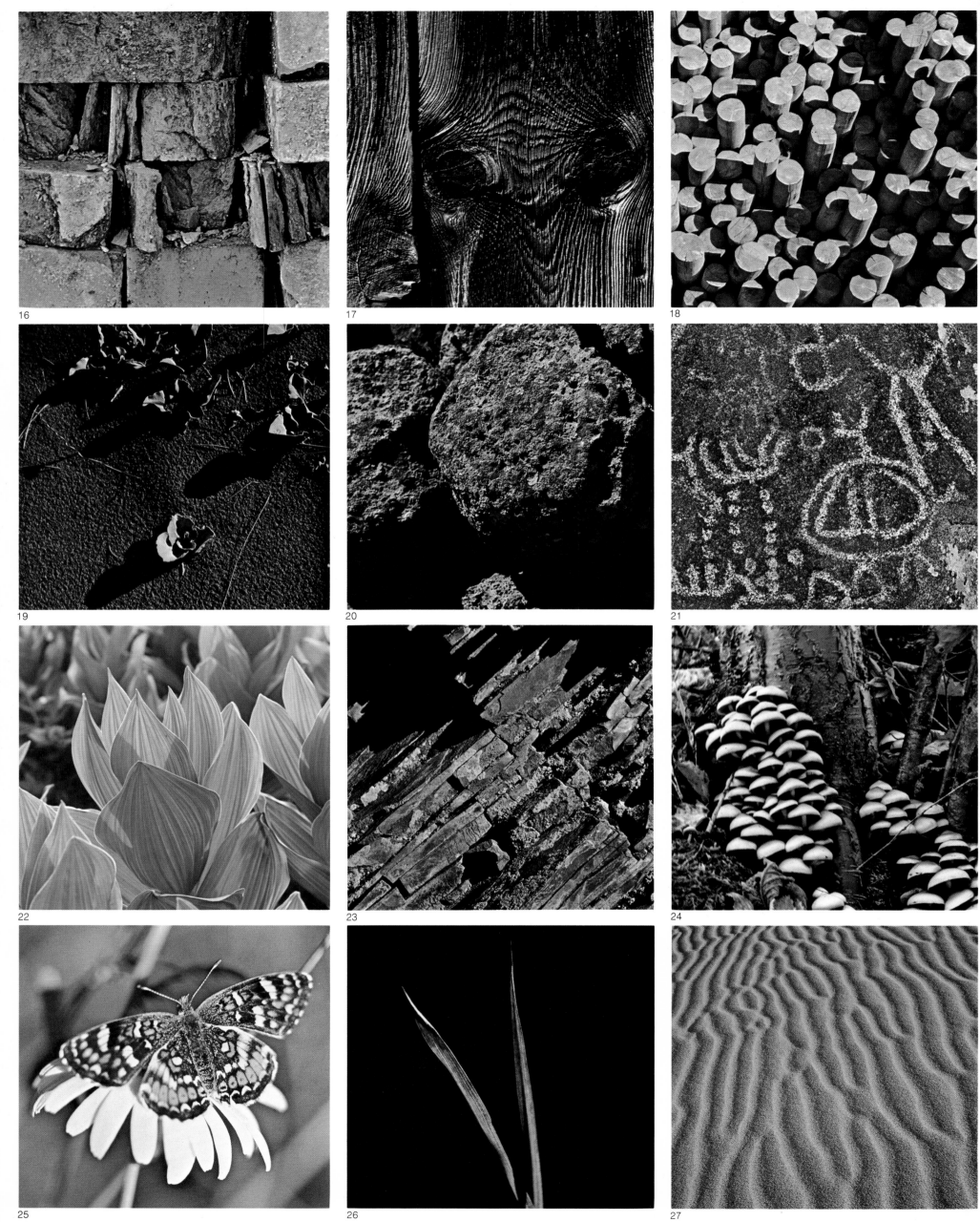

16

17

18

19

20

21

22

23

24

25

26

27

202

PHOTO INDEX AND CREDITS

When the word got out that an illustrated folio book on Idaho was under way, we were deluged with photographs, from 35mm to 8″ x 10″ transparencies, from amateur and professional alike, and from all over the United States. In the end, we reviewed over 10,000 submissions by over 100 photographers, finally choosing those listed below. It was a difficult selection process.

We had to reject an enormous number of superb scenes and subjects, not because they were bad photographs, but because they did not fit our color balance, design, or the story line and feeling that we were trying to create in communicating what Idaho and its people are all about.

Many of the photographs in this book are the results of great effort on the part of one or more individuals over a long period of time. The variety is, I think, one of the things which sets the book apart. The fact that one person may have only one photo in this book and another may have twenty is not necessarily related to the quality of the photo or skill of the photographer. In some cases, we selected a less dramatic shot because it balanced our layout or our story more effectively.

We are grateful indeed to all those who submitted material for review, whether finally purchased or not. Their patience in permitting us to keep some of their photographs for extended periods of time during the complex selection and layout process is sincerely appreciated.

— Bob Beatty

TEXTURES

Alphabetical List of Photographers Whose Works Appear In This Book

ARNOLD, Lance
BAKER, Spike
BAUER, Erwin A.
BEATTY, David C.
BEATTY, Robert O.
BENNATI, Guido
BENSON, Pat
BENSON, Woodward
BLEDSOE, James
BOEHLKE, David
BOLES, Jan
BONMAN, Al
BURTCH, Margaret
CHENEY, Clinton

COLLIE, Mark
COOPER, Edward
CURTIS, A. B.
DAVIS, Duane
DAVIS, Mary
DAY, Ernest
DEMETRY, Robert
DOUGLAS, Dixie
DREWEIN, Rod
FITZWATER, William D.
FRAZIER, David
GARRETT, Duane
GLOVER, Neil
GRANGE, William

GREGORY, Ralph
GRIFFITHS, Henry
HAGDORN, William
HALL, Ross
HANKS, Marvin
HAUCK, Eldon
HENDREN, Aleen
HENDREN, R. L., Sr.
HIDY, V. S.
HILLIARD, Stanley
HORNER, R. B.
HORNOCKER, Maurice
HUFF, Howard
HUSER, Verne

JOHNSON, Dan
JOHNSON, Eileen
KORTE, Erich
LEEGE, Thomas
LEONARD, Joe
LINDHOLM, Fred
LOMBARD, Ernest
MASLOWSKI, Karl
MASON, F. R.
McNEEL, Jack
MEINERS, William
MORACHE, Martel
MULLINS, William
NASKALI, Richard

NEIDNER, Kenn
NELSON, Morlan W.
NELSON, Norm
NORRIE, Ken
PETERSON, Ernst
POE, Coy
POWELL, Kelly
RODERICK, Dave
ROTTIER, Jack
SCHEER, Charles
SCHWARTZ, George
SHADDUCK, Louise
SLOWIK, Michael
STATES, Gary

SUMNER, David
SUMNER, Judy
TALLON, James
TRUEBLOOD, Ellen
TRUEBLOOD, Ted
TUTTLE, Ralph
UIHLEIN, Reven
URBAN, Karl
WALKER, Kyle
WILLIAMS, Jack
WYMAN, Julia

Other Sources:

Boy Scouts of America
Idaho Department of Parks
Idaho Historical Society
Idaho Mining Association
Montague, Marion (Collection)
National Aeronautics and
    Space Administration
Smithsonian Institution
U.S. Geological Survey
U.S. National Park Service
Ye Galleon Press

* * *

ACKNOWLEDGMENTS

Acknowledgments are tricky because someone may be inadvertently left out. *Everyone* who helps an author/editor put a book together is indispensable, but some are a shade more indispensable than others.

There are no "last, but not leasts" or priority lists connected with the immensely complex process of putting this book on Idaho together; but there are certainly some without whose dedication it could not have been done on time — and that includes some who were paid for their efforts and some who were not.

The total production staff for this book consisted of designer Dale Ott, and my assistant, Carol Clapp. Dale's superior work is self-evident. Carol, in addition to typing manuscripts and correspondence, kept inventory records and handled the packaging and mailing of the thousands of photographs submitted, and attended to countless production details. My sincere thanks go also to the following:

For help in proofreading — Louise Bray of the bank staff, and Louise Beatty of my fireside "staff," and Jeanne Johnson of Caxton's. Several bank personnel were most helpful with supplies and equipment.

For great assistance in historical research — the entire staff of the Idaho Historical Society, but especially Museum Director Arthur Hart, Fred Walters, and Ms. Hilma Peterson; Jim Davis of the Idaho State Library staff; and the genial ladies at the reference desk of the Boise Public Library.

For information on a variety of questions related to Idaho fauna and flora — Martel Morache, Supervisor of Conservation Education; and Dick Norell, Game Bird Supervisor, Idaho Department of Fish and Game; Richard Naskali, Assistant Professor, Botany, University of Idaho, Moscow; and Dr. Donald Obee, Chairman of the Department of Biological Sciences, Boise State University.

For assistance in obtaining and identifying special photographs — Ms. Dorine Goertzen, Idaho Department of Commerce and Development, and Editor of *Incredible Idaho;* Ms. Phyllis Montague of Clarkston, Washington; and many members of the Boise Camera Club, some of whose works appear herein.

For data on pictographs and petroglyphs — Earl H. Swanson, Director of The Museum of Archaeology, Idaho State University; and Ms. Nelle Tobias of McCall.

For background on the use of natural foods by Idaho pioneers and Indians — Carl Brown of McCall.

For special help on historical facts relating to the Owyhee plateau — the Owyhee County Historical Society at Murphy.

For dedication to quality and long hours to meet deadlines — all the fine folks at the Caxton Printers in Caldwell, but especially to Dale Morgan, color department; Tom Gill, pressman; George Stuchbery, bindery foreman; Bob Killebrew, composition department; and Lindy Johnson, plant superintendent, who cheerfully coordinated these production processes under considerable pressure at times. I cannot overlook, either, the fine spirit of cooperation displayed by Bill Krell and his associates at Sweeney, Krist, and Dimm, Portland.

A special word of thanks is due to Pat Benson (photographer) and Otis, the very much alive golden eagle, posed in his natural habitat on a Snake River canyon, who graces our dust jacket. Otis was taken from his nest and trained by Morley Nelson, his owner, seven years ago. He has become something of a motion picture and television star, though this is his first book appearance. His "royalty" for the job was a fresh rabbit's foot, thigh included. The rest of us rubbed it a little first!

And finally, my especial admiration goes to Tom Frye, who left us alone, and without whose foresight and faith this book could never have come into being.

— **Bob Beatty**

BIBLIOGRAPHY

The editor and publisher have made every effort to trace the ownership of all copyrighted material and to secure permission from copyright holders of such material as required. In the event of any question arising as to the use of any material, the publisher and the editor, while expressing regret for inadvertent error, will be pleased to make the necessary corrections in any future printings. We are grateful to the following authors, publishers, publications, and agents for use of selected excerpts or general reference works indicated below or in the text:

ARMSTRONG, Margaret *Field Book of Western Wild Flowers* ©1915 by C. P. Putnam Sons, New York, N.Y.

ARNOLD, Lloyd R. *High On the Wild With Hemingway* ©1968 by The Caxton Printers, Ltd., Caldwell, Idaho.

BARBER, Floyd R. and MARTIN, Dan W. *Idaho in the Pacific Northwest* ©1956 by The Caxton Printers, Ltd., Caldwell, Idaho.

BARLETT, Des and Jen "Beavers — Nature's Aquatic Engineers" *National Geographic*, Vol. 145, No. 5, ©1974 by National Geographic Society.

BAUER, Donald E. *Ghost Towns and Back Roads* ©1971 by the Stackpole Co., Harrisburg, Pennsylvania.

BECKWITH, John A. *Gem Minerals of Idaho* ©1972 by The Caxton Printers, Ltd., Caldwell, Idaho.

BENÉT, Stephen Vincent "Western Star" and "Ode to Walt Whitman" Holt, Rinehart and Winston, ©1943 by Stephen Vincent Benét; © renewed ©1971 by Rachel Benét Lewis, Thomas C. Benét, and Stephanie Benét Mahin; quotations reprinted by permission of Brandt and Brandt.

BENNING, Esther "Gordon's Retreat" *Incredible Idaho*, Vol. 4, No. 3, 1972.

CAREY, Samuel *Wild Flowers at a Glance* ©1950 by Pellegrini & Cudahy, New York, N.Y.

CAVAGNARO, David Paraphrases on pages 49 and 68: of short passages from pages 87 and 152 of *Living Water* ©1971 by American West Publishing Co., Palo Alto, Calif.

CLEMENS, Samuel *Life on the Mississippi* 1883

CROWELL, Grace Noll "Keep Some Green Memory Alive" from *Poems of Inspiration and Courage* ©1950 by Harper and Row Publishers, Inc., New York, N.Y.

DEVOE, Alan *This Fascinating Animal World* ©1951 by McGraw-Hill Book Co., New York, N.Y.

DRISCOLL, Ann Nillson *They Came to a Ridge* ©1970 by A. N. Driscoll, printed by the News Review Publishing Co., Inc., Moscow, Idaho.

ELLIOTT & CO. *History of the Idaho Territory*, 1884 Ye Galleon Press Edition (Glen C. Adams), Fairfield, Washington, 1973.

ELLIS, William S. "High Stepping Idaho" *National Geographic*, Vol. 143, No. 3, March, 1973. ©1973 Nat'l. Geographic Society.

FEDERAL WRITERS PROJECT, WPA *Idaho, A Guide in Word and Picture* ©1937 by The Caxton Printers, Ltd., Caldwell, Idaho; and *Idaho Encyclopedia* ©1938 by Idaho Secretary of State, printed by The Caxton Printers, Ltd., Caldwell, Idaho.

FLEMING, Lora *Interprofiles* Sales Building Promotions, Pocatello, Idaho. ©1973 by Lora Fleming.

FLEXNER, Hortense "Immortality," ©by Houghton Mifflin Co., Boston, Massachusetts, date unknown.

GEM STATE AUTHORS GUILD *Starlight and Syringa* Gateway Printers, Inc., 1959.

GLEN, R. T. *Ghost Towns and Mining Camps of Idaho* ©by Alturas Enterprises, Boise, Idaho.

GLENN, T. R. and Cubit, Jack *Idaho Treasure Tales and Treasure Trails* ©by Alturas Enterprises, Boise, Idaho.

GRAYSON, David *Adventures of David Grayson* ©1925 by Doubleday-Page and Co., Garden City, N.Y.

GREAT WEST SERIES *The Magnificent Rockies* ©1973 by the American West Publishing Co., Palo Alto, California.

GULICK, Bill *Snake River Country* ©1971 by The Caxton Printers, Ltd., Caldwell, Idaho.

HAILEY, John *The History of Idaho* printed by Syms York Co., Boise, Idaho, 1910.

HANLEY, Mike and LUCIA, Ellis *Owyhee Trails* ©1973 by The Caxton Printers, Ltd., Caldwell, Idaho.

HEMINGWAY, Mary "Ernest's Idaho and Mine" *World Magazine*, November, 1972. ©1972 by Mary Hemingway.

IRVING, Washington *Adventures of Captain Bonneville* 1837; and *Astoria* 1836.

JOHNSON, F. D. *Native Trees of Idaho* Bulletin 289, Idaho Agricultural Extension Service, Boise, Idaho, 1966.

JOSEPHY, Alvin M., Jr. *The Great West* ©1965 by American Heritage Publishing Co., New York, N.Y.

KORTRIGHT, F. H. *The Ducks, Geese and Swans of North America* ©1943 by American Wildlife Institute, Washington, D.C.

LEOPOLD, Aldo *Round River* ©1953 by Oxford University Press, Inc., New York, N.Y.

LITTLEFIELD, Carroll and FERGUSON, Denzel "The Sandhill Crane — Avian Spectacle" ©Oct., 1970 by *Pacific Search Magazine*.

MIDMORE, Joe *Middle Fork History* ©1973 by Harrah's Club, Inc., Reno, Nevada.

MIGHELL, Marjorie "Beauty in Our Own Backyard" from *Love and Laughter*, ©1967 by Marjorie Holmes Mighell, Doubleday and Co., Inc., New York, N.Y.

MORGAN, Ann Haven *Field Book of Ponds and Streams* ©1930 by G. P. Putnam Sons, New York, N.Y.

MUIR, John *The Treasures of the Yosemite* ©1970 by Lewis Osborne, printed by Lane Magazine and Book Co., Menlo Park, California.

NELSON, E. W. *Wild Animals of North America* ©1930 by National Geographic Society, Washington, D.C.

NORTON, Boyd *The Snake Wilderness* ©1972 by Sierra Club Books, San Francisco, California.

OSBORNE, Kelsey Ramey *Peaceful Conquest* printed by Beattie and Co., Portland, Oregon, 1955.

PATTERSON, Robert L. *The Sage Grouse in Wyoming* Wyoming Game and Fish Commission, 1952.

PRATHER, Hugh *I Touch the Earth and the Earth Touches Me* ©1972 by Hugh Prather, Doubleday and Co., Garden City, N.Y.; and *Notes To Myself* ©1970 by Real People Press, Moab, Utah.

ROSS, Sylvia and SAVAGE, Carl *Idaho Earth Science* Idaho Department of Mines and Geology, 1967.

RUSSELL, Terry and Renny Material on pages 35, 54 and 130 from *On the Loose* ©1967 by Sierra Club.

SLICKPOO, Allen P., Sr. *Cultural History of the Nez Perce* Vol. I, ©1973 by Nez Perce Tribes of Idaho; and *Nez Perce Legends* ©1972 by Nez Perce Tribes of Idaho.

SPARLING, Wayne *Southern Idaho Ghost Towns* ©1974 by The Caxton Printers, Ltd., Caldwell, Idaho.

VOLLMER, John P. *Illustrated History of North Idaho* printed by Western Historical Publishing Co., 1903.

WEIS, Norman D. *Ghost Towns of the Northwest* ©1972 by The Caxton Printers, Ltd., Caldwell, Idaho.

WELLS, Merle W. *Idaho – A Student's Guide To Localized History* Teachers College, Columbia University, N.Y., 1965.

WETMORE, Alexander *Water, Prey and Game Birds of North America* ©1965, National Geographic Society, Washington, D.C.

WHITMAN, Walt "Song of Myself," 1855

* * * * *

The Idaho Almanac, Department of Commerce and Development, printed by Syms York Co., Boise, Idaho, 1963.

Idaho Yesterdays, Vol. 1-17, Quarterly Journal of the Idaho Historical Society, Boise.

Reference Series, The Idaho Historical Society, Boise.

Standard Reference Map and Guide to Idaho, ©1972 by Rand-McNally and Co., Chicago, Illinois.

Sunset Travel Guide to Idaho, ©1972 by Lane Books, Menlo Park, California.